Notes
from a Farmer

Notes from a Farmer

Letters and Observations by McWilliam Davis

TATE PUBLISHING
AND ENTERPRISES, LLC

Notes from a Farmer
Copyright © 2013 by McWilliam Davis. All rights reserved.

No part of this publication may be reproduced, stored in a retrieval system or transmitted in any way by any means, electronic, mechanical, photocopy, recording or otherwise without the prior permission of the author except as provided by USA copyright law.

Scriptures taken from the Holy Bible, New International Version®, NIV®. Copyright © 1973, 1978, 1984 by Biblica, Inc.™ Used by permission of Zondervan. All rights reserved worldwide. www.zondervan.com

The opinions expressed by the author are not necessarily those of Tate Publishing, LLC.

Published by Tate Publishing & Enterprises, LLC
127 E. Trade Center Terrace | Mustang, Oklahoma 73064 USA
1.888.361.9473 | www.tatepublishing.com

Tate Publishing is committed to excellence in the publishing industry. The company reflects the philosophy established by the founders, based on Psalm 68:11,
"The Lord gave the word and great was the company of those who published it."

Book design copyright © 2013 by Tate Publishing, LLC. All rights reserved.
Cover design by Jacie Carvajal
Interior design by Honeylette Pino

Published in the United States of America

ISBN: 978-1-62854-809-9
1. Biography & Autobiography / Personal Memoirs
2. Biography & Autobiography / Cultural Heritage
13.09.23

Acknowledgment

The family of McWilliam Davis is grateful to the many people who have so patiently and eagerly awaited the completion of this project. Without their support, this compilation culled from an overwhelming trove of columns, letters, stories, and observations, would perhaps have taken another decade to complete. Special thanks to Kay Davis and her granddaughter, Nicole Davis, for photograph selections, to Assunta Martin and Jess Davis for their work with the content material, and to Tanya Kennedy, Calleen Davis, Augie Martin, Angie and Tony Rincon, Becca Davis, Eli Kennedy, and Carrie Hulett for their ongoing support and patience. We also extend our deep gratitude to Don and Virginia Hall. Their encouragement and generosity convinced Mac and Kay to spend more time writing and to buy their first computer/word processor. Kudos to Dennis Knox for his gentle, yet persistent, urging to complete this project for all to enjoy. Many thanks also to the Fairview community, the staff of the Fairview Republican, and all of our many relatives and friends whose love for Mac's writings inspired this endeavor.

We also thank the staff at Tate Publishing for their efforts in bringing this project to a successful completion.

Dedication

In Loving Memory of Dad

Contents

Foreword 8

Notes from a Farmer 11

Observations and Musings 84

Devil Lanes 126

Hawk Observations 148

More about Hawks 151

Belize Adventures 156

Letters from Mac 171

Munich and World War II Memories 215

Poems by Mac Davis 236

Commentaries About McWilliam Davis 246

Foreword

Mac

by Kay Davis

Profile of Dad

Keep a low profile; these words best describe the way he runs his life. He is a strong man, a gentle man, a thinking man. He struggles at times to protect his low-key image.

Known for quiet, thoughtful, good judgment, Mac has served his community and his family well. He is a role model to many—men, women, and children—when asked, and only when asked, he gives advice carefully, weighing each thought.

His life is the embodiment of all the sage sayings a grandmother says and all the Aesop's Fables and the golden rule. He is a good man—he is loved.

He is a voracious reader, savoring each book and article, every account of history or individual; and rolling facts and tales around in his mind much like when he rolled good whiskey in his mouth in the drinking days.

He is a writer, a word-pinching writer. He is a perfectionist in his writing, poring over each phrase, mulling over his repertoire of words—picking, choosing, changing.

He used to write a column for the local weekly paper in the hometown he was born and raised in. One week, there was an overload of material for the opinion page. The layout person said everything would fit if she could omit two paragraphs of his column. The editor screamed, "Don't touch his column! There's not one excess word in it."

He is a farmer, a careful farmer, a meticulous, planning, thrifty farmer. He has been a geologist, a mapmaker, a surveyor, a soldier, but being a farmer is what he likes better than all the rest. He meditates while he is on his tractor. He observes nature from his tractor. He comes home with tales of hawks, rabbits, killdeer, coyotes, and gulls. His rows are straight.

An absentminded person, he goes through red lights, stops at green lights, answers a question three minutes after it has been asked; his mind, light-years away, pondering heavy thoughts or humorous happenings.

He had his idiosyncrasies. He ties his socks in knots before he puts them in the hamper. He likes his pancakes right side up and his apples peeled from the top.

Growing up during the depression, he had a Jean Shepherd kind of childhood. His experiences and escapades in a small town neighborhood shaped his life as did being the son of loving, no-nonsense parents whose guiding lines had to be, "Use it up, wear it out, make it do, or do without."

He went through World War II with no physical wounds but with many hairy experiences. He was in Germany when they opened up Dachau. He married a German girl. They came to the United States and enrolled at the University of Oklahoma. They had two children. They divorced, and he remarried and had two more children.

Notes from a Farmer

Writing a column for the *Fairview Republican*

For several years during the 1980s, McWilliam Davis, better known as "Mac" by friends and family, wrote a column for the *Fairview Republican*, the only local newspaper published in Fairview, Oklahoma. The columns are a collection of observations, stories, and comments inspired by events and people in the community. Although his wife, Kay Davis, was employed as a local reporter and wrote many featured stories for the newspaper, Mac never worked for the *Fairview Republican*. His columns were an entertaining addition donated to the paper and eagerly anticipated by an ever increasing number of regular readers.

A short article accompanying Mac's obituary in the *Fairview Republican* commented, "His favorite gifts, both to give and to receive, were books. He was a scholar, reading avidly and was very knowledgeable on a wide range of subjects. History was a particular favorite, and he could recount stories from any period." Mac wrote a weekly column "Notes from a Farmer" for several years for this newspaper. His stories were entertaining, thoughtful, and anticipated by his many fans. His letters to family and friends were just as eagerly welcomed, and his character came through as clearly on e-mails as on a hand-written note.

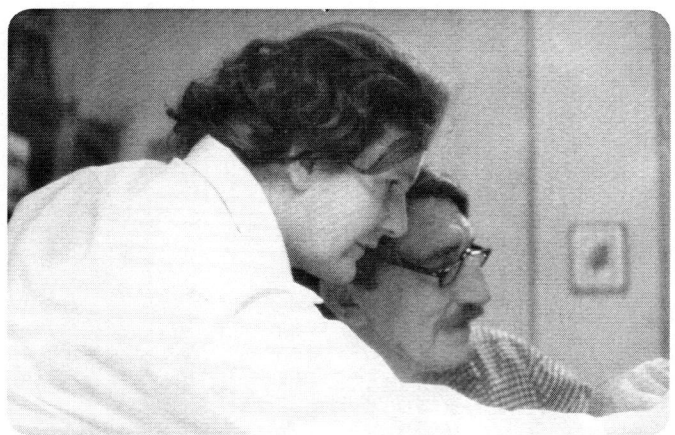

Kay and Mac reviewing an article for the *Fairview Republican*

An Afternoon in the Courthouse

January 15, 1981

Never look a gift horse in the mouth. That is an old adage that should be taken with a grain of salt. If anyone offers to sell you a valuable article for a give-away price, don't buy it until you find out how heavy it is.

Last week, the Major County Historical Society was the successful bidder on a piece of obsolete machinery owned by the county. For reasons I have forgotten, the chore of removing this thing to safe storage fell to me.

I should have known better. In the first place, the Major County Historical Society doesn't own any storage facilities. It doesn't own much of anything. As far as I know, it is practically defunct. In the second place, the minute I saw what had been bought, I should have returned to my farm and disconnected the telephone.

For a sealed bid of one United States dollar, the county commissioners turned over to the Major County Historical Society a photocopying instrument located in the county clerk's office. This apparatus is ten feet long, seven feet high, thirty-two inches wide and weighs maybe 1,200 pounds. Maybe it weighs a ton. I don't know.

There is little to be gained in explaining how this monstrous machine came to rest midway down the last flight of stairs in the county courthouse. Lodged it was, stuck between the ceiling and the steps, wedged, immoveable by any amount of strong arms that would get around it.

There are people who will tell you all kinds of lies about this operation, and there are countless people who would have planned the job differently. The truth of the matter is that there was no plan. It all happened just like a blizzard or a hail storm happens. It was an act of God.

The comments of the passersby during the three or four hours this priceless machine sat in the stairway were interesting. Several folks recommended a cutting torch. Dozens of them mumbled the same dumb questions. Why didn't you take it apart? What are you going to do now? Betty Wallace suggested we just brick up the stairwell and forget the whole thing. That appealed to me since the courthouse does have an elevator and walking up all those steps is bad for old folks anyway.

Along in the shank-end of the afternoon, after the county's lifting crew went home (man, did I envy them), Dallas Womack remarked, "You need Hank Martens."

I coaxed Hank Martens from under a house he was shoring up on Tenth Street and he came to the courthouse. He analyzed the problem. "We need a tractor with a front-end loader and a good driver," he said.

A tractor inside the courthouse?

That's the way we got it out. Vernon Fast drove in the west door with his tractor, and after about two-hundred little tiny maneuvers, he skidded the thing out onto the courthouse lawn.

I leave to your imagination all the details of this story that I have left out. Through the generosity of David Martens, the machine now sits safe, dry, secure, and all wrapped up in the northwest corner of his warehouse near the airport. In the future, I suppose some ambitious souls will have the wit and wherewithal to put this instrument on display in some museum. I wish them well.

Alumni Report

July 23, 1981

Dear Editor:

The reason you have not heard from me for some weeks is not on account of the pay. The pay is okay. The compensation for my scribbling seems about equal to its worth.

The real reason for my silence is a direct result of my wife's ambitious nature. She has kept me so busy bringing in the sheaves and toiling in the soil and fixing the plumbing and taking care of the cows that I have just not had time for anything serious and worthwhile.

I did get hold of some information at the recent school reunion which will surely be of great interest to the editor of a newspaper.

After visiting with scores of alumni over a long weekend, it became obvious to me that the alumni of this community have produced a crop of children and grandchildren (especially, grandchildren) that are far and away the most beautiful, intelligent, and all-around superior folks the world has ever been blessed with. It is probable that in the near future, historians, philosophers, psychologists, and theologians will be coming here in droves to find out what it is about our air and water that has caused this sudden blooming of civilization. You should prepare yourself for this.

As for my own class, I was pleased to discover, after discreet inquiry, that not a single member of the class is presently in the penitentiary or even under serious indictment.

Also, I can report that from a material point of view, everyone seems to have done moderately well. All those who came to the reunion got here with enough money to get back home. We didn't have to take up a collection for anybody.

Babies

Reading to the grandkids

April 8, 1982

It has been a while since I had anything to do with baby people. But I am getting back into the swing of things.

About 4:30 on the morning of April Fool's Day, our daughter woke us up and announced that she and her husband were on their way to the hospital. The time had come.

I wished her well and rolled over to sleep. My wife elbowed me in the ribs and said, "Put the coffee on, feed the cows, get ready, she expects us to be there."

It was the first time I had been informed of my important role in the business at hand.

We got to the hospital at 8 a.m. and along about 7 p.m., grandson Elijah announced his presence in this world. He was certainly welcomed.

During the long day, I did not have much to do. A grandfather is not a very useful member of the birthing team. I read the newspapers, looked at the babies in the nursery, talked with the nurses, the aides, the janitors, and people in the lounge. I ate breakfast, lunch, and supper in the cafeteria, drank a gallon or so of coffee and seriously contemplated weaning myself from cigarettes.

I recalled the births of my four children. (My first child was delivered in a military hospital in Germany by a sergeant in the medical corps of the US Army. The sergeant was good at patching bullet holes, but he was not adept in birthing. It was a terrible experience).

I thought about the years that have passed. How my children have grown. How short the time has been.

As the day wore on, I marveled at my calmness. I was grateful for the efficiency and gentleness of the staff. I never worried about anything. Finally it was over. The mother was well, the baby was healthy. It was a good day.

Our daughter-in-law has yet another grandchild due in three weeks. I can wait. I have the patience of Job. I am definitely getting into the swing of it all.

Bad Cold

January 26, 1984

I am looking forward to tomorrow. Tomorrow will be the seventh day I have endured a bad cold. Tomorrow I will be well.

When you start hacking and snorting with the onset of a cold, everyone tells you same thing. If you don't take any medicine, it takes seven days for a cold to run its course. If you take medicine for the cold, it takes a week to run its course. That is true folk wisdom learned from centuries of mankind doping himself with everything from boiled lizard livers, to Dristan and Comtrex, trying to cure himself of the common cold. It can't be done.

I know that but I never fail to fight a cold as hard as I can. I take hot showers, sleep late, and go to bed early. I moan and groan a lot, drink quarts of fruit juice and brothy soups, eat sparingly, and even cut down on my smoking. I eat aspirin and Dristan tablets, and ingest colorful capsules full of little time bombs. Sometimes I concentrate on the old folk remedies like sassafras tea and bicarbonate of soda in warm water. Someone even tried kerosene and sugar one time, but I don't recommend that. It will make you sick.

Hope, I think is what encourages me to take medicines for a cold. Even though they have never done me much good, I always have hope that I will chance upon the right combination of dope that will cure the common cold. Think of that! And then, too, it gives me something to do. Instead of just moaning and groaning, blowing my nose, and coughing, I can keep an eye on the clock to see if it is time to try something else.

Basketball Trip

I was sitting in the Hiway Cafe one afternoon awhile back, sipping coffee with some other loafers, when the high school activities bus rolled by. It was loaded with young folks on their way to somewhere to do their best for the Fairview Yellow Jackets. The bus had just been cleaned and washed and it sparkled in the afternoon sun. The huge dual driving wheels still glistened from their recent washing and the motor hummed with a powerful purr. It was uplifting and wondrous to behold. It reminded me of a story Mush McCue told me one time.

Around 1934 to 1935, Fred Irion was superintendent of the school system. The annual school budget was about $17,000 and Mr. Irion counted pennies and nickels like a banker figuring interest. One day, he handed Mutt Herring, the Yellow Jackets' coach, a letter from the Alva school district. It was an invitation to a basketball game. "You can go if you can get them up there," is what he told the coach.

The basketball players were elated. They practiced hard and washed up their uniforms. Some of them got new laces for their tennis shoes. They were ready. The coach wasn't.

Insufficient transportation was the problem. Coach Herring had his own coupe in which he could carry the basketball gear and two skinny players. He had one car volunteered for the trip, but he needed another one. Both the A team and the B team were scheduled to play.

So he went to the boss, Fritz Irion, who called downtown to the Dodge Motor Company. And Jake Boehs, the manager, loaned the school a good used Model-T Ford sedan which held six basketball players. It had wood spoke wheels, painted red. The trip was on.

The roads were not all paved. It rained. Highway signs were not what they are today. Near Avard, the Model-T missed a turn and lost the other two cars. What with one thing and another part of the team arrived late. But not too late, the games had just started. An eventful trip.

The Yellow Jackets won both games (we think). Late at night, two of the cars loaded up again and started back to Fairview. Coach Herring tarried awhile in Alva visiting old friends.

The trip back was also eventful. The cars got separated going through Carmen. South of Cleo Springs, the Model-T blew out a tire. The spare was flat. Nothing to do but keep rolling. At the river bridge, the flat tire finally flayed to pieces. They bumped along on the rim. South of Orienta, the wood spokes scattered in the road. The rim collapsed and the Model-T sagged down, dead, four miles from home.

Reality is reality. The basketball trip continued. The boys got out and dragged the heap off the road into the ditch, buttoned up their coats, turned up their collars, and trudged on in to town. That's about the end of the story.

Except—the two boys riding with Mutt Herring when he came upon the scene a couple of hours later said he got out and stood studying the broken wheel for a while. Then he shrugged his shoulders, crawled back into the coupe, and mumbled half to himself, "Well, old Fritz will just have to squeeze the general fund for the cost of that wheel."

Bellmon Claims Plans Phony

September 18, 1980

> *Truth: A commodity, the supply of which always exceeds the demand.*
>
> —Ambrose Bierce (circa 1910)

The campaigning tempo for the national elections coming up in a few weeks has increased to almost the shrill yelling stage. Henry Bellmon, who is quitting his job as US Senator next term and is not running for anything, made a speech three weeks ago which has brought to my mind Mr. Ambrose Bierce's definition of the word "truth."

Both the Republican and the Democrat party have announced general plans of government which will reduce taxes and halt inflation. Mr. Bellmon said in his speech that neither one of these plans will do any such thing. He was blunter than that. He said both plans are *phony*.

Now, Mr. Bellmon seemingly has no ax to grind; he is highly respected in Congress and enjoys a national reputation for hard work and stability.

So what happened after he labeled both the Republican and the Democrat tax-reducing plans phony?

Well, nothing much. A couple of brief remarks about it on the next day's newscast and that will be the end of it. No politician or statesman spoke up to refute him or support him. No columnist wrote to analyze his remarks. He was, as far as I've seen or heard, ignored.

I think Mr. Bellmon put more truth on the market than the market can handle.

Boom Town Tale

October 23, 1980

We aren't exactly an oil boom town yet, but we are surely moving away from being just a plain old wheat and cow town. The through-town traffic is getting to be about as challenging every day now as it used to be only at harvest time.

There are a lot of stories about boom towns and how they started. In the October issue of the *Smithsonian* magazine, there is a spellbinding story about how the great Southern California oil boom developed eighty odd years ago. Here is how it began.

In 1892, Ed Doheny, a down-on-his-luck gold prospector, stood in Westlake Park a mile from downtown Los Angeles looking at a natural tar pit. He deduced that it was a dried up spring. An oil spring. The city of Los Angeles sits on a pool of oil. He decided and went straight to work.

He and his partner bought a vacant lot in a residential area on Glendale Boulevard and started digging a hole with spades. They dug down 155 feet. Then they made a giant punch out of a tree trunk, rigged up some block and tackles, and by raising and dropping this drill bit, struck oil at 460 feet. It flowed forty barrels a day.

Now, if that is not an example of self-confidence and perseverance, we are not likely to find one.

Boots

> *About eighty percent of all western boots are made in Tennessee...*
>
> —*The Sunday Oklahoman*, February 15, 1981.

I would guess the other 20 percent are made in Texas and Taiwan.

The article in *The Oklahoman* goes to some length explaining the recent upsurge in western wear clothes fashions. It goes to further lengths trying to explain the great demand for western (cowboy) boots.

"The popularity of western wear," the article says, "represents a search for fundamental values. The cowboy look is the only authentic costume the US has."

I don't believe that. Present day western wear and cowboy boots may be a kind of costume all right, but authentic, they are not. More cattle have been kicked in the ribs with a shoe than ever got kicked with a boot. I think the typical high-heeled boot, as we know it was pretty rare footwear in the old west.

Most of our ideas about authentic western wear come from TV and the movies, and I'm pretty sure they are off base. Western movies usually involve flamboyant outlaws and relentless lawmen of the early days, the type of folks you would surely expect to be dressed in western wear.

I have seen copies of two photographs of Butch Cassidy, the infamous Wyoming outlaw of the 1890s. In one picture he is wearing high-topped, side-buttoned shoes. In the other photo, he is wearing knee-high, laced-up boots.

Frank Canton was a US marshal who helped clear out the bad guys in early-day Oklahoma. He later organized and headed the first Oklahoma Militia in the 1920s. A photograph of him shows a fellow with a walrus moustache wearing a Russian type fur cap and an overcoat buttoned from his throat to his ankles. I can't tell what he has on his feet. Certain it is, he was dressed for a blizzard.

George Nichols, a writer for *Harper's Magazine* in 1867 interviewed James Butler "Wild Bill" Hickok. In discussing this man killer's dress, Nichols describes Wild Bill's large sombrero, his long-tailed leather frock (whatever that is), and his bright-yellow moccasins.

In 1895, posses from Major County and surrounding counties finally overtook the outlaws Dick Yeager and Isaac Black. I don't know what Mr. Black was wearing when they shot him down in a cornfield near Longdale, but Marquis James, the historian, reports that Yeager, when captured in another cornfield near Hennessey, was wearing one shoe and one boot.

Bridge Planks

October 1, 1981

About twenty years ago, I bought a used one-thousand-bushel steel grain bin at a farm sale. When the time came to move it, I went for advice to a neighbor who knows how to do things like that.

"You will need a tractor, a log chain, a jack, and two stout bridge planks," he said. "Raise the granary a few inches, slide the planks under it, lash on the log chain and skid the thing home with the tractor. Nothing to it."

I had everything but the bridge planks. Who has bridge planks? The county has bridge planks. I got hold of John Shewey, my favorite county commissioner, to see if he could help me out. He could and he did. We went out to the county's material yard, and John loaned me two real solid bridge planks and I went home to move the granary.

I have been thinking about that deal lately and I am getting worried. With all of the hullabaloo going on about Oklahoma's county commissioners, I am beginning to suffer a terrible guilt complex.

You see, I never did get around to taking the planks back. They lay out behind the barn for several years and different neighbors borrowed them for one purpose or another and I just plain lost track of them. I don't know where they are. They may even be worn out by now.

I am getting kind of spooky and wary-like around strangers. I am afraid the FBI may be onto our trail.

Of course, John retired several years ago. In fact, he died several years ago. He is safe. But I am still here. And I am busy. Man, am I busy. I don't have any time to visit with FBI agents.

So, I am herewith sending out a kind of general plea: If anybody, anywhere, knows anything about those two bridge planks, please let me know about it. I want to get them back to the county yard before the feds inventory the place.

Bugs and High Tech

January 10, 1985

A farmer's work is mostly war against weeds, insects, and predators. One of the first jobs I can remember was picking bugs off potato plants. And at the age of three, I almost did myself in drinking fly poison from a saucer sitting on the window sill in the cow barn.

Through the years, knowledge has increased and methods have changed but the war remains. Today we have powerful tractors and high speed machines. We have pesticides and herbicides with names a foot and half long. And the fight goes on with insects, worms, aphids, fungi, molds, nematodes, and critters yet unnamed.

We struggle with noxious weeds from Canada, Africa, Russia, and China. Fire ants are moving up from Central America. Killer bees are buzzing in from Brazil. Who knows what is coming down on us from the Polar Regions?

Politicians, generals, and university folk talk about star wars and a high tech society. They are busy designing and producing sophisticated devices that will keep the electronic and computer industries humming.

I hope somebody somewhere is thinking about Mother Nature and bugs.

Let me tell you a funny story I heard during Christmas holidays. The F-16 fighter plane is one of the most complex machines ever built. It is built here in the United States and sold all over the world to friendly governments whom we hope will remain friendly. The machines cost twenty-two million dollars each.

There are teams of engineers and technicians who monitor every minute of every flight of every plane. They watch for malfunctions so they can be corrected or at least explained.

Egypt has F-16 fighter planes. One of the greatest causes of malfunction of Egyptian planes turns out to be rats. Rats crawl up in the planes at night and chew on the wiring and eat the tubing. A very difficult problem. One suggested solution was to furnish each plane with four cats and a ferret. The brass considered that a very bad joke.

Bats are the problem in Pakistan. In one area patrolled by F-16s, great swarms of bats flew up every evening from their caves and got sucked into the jets. At dawn, the bats returning to their caves also got sucked into the jets.

The problem was easily solved. They quit flying the planes over bat caves in the evening and early morning.

On a base in the southwestern United States, it was little green worms that messed up the plane. Caterpillars took residence in the air tube that activates the thing-a-majig that calculates the speed of the plane.

And that's how one butterfly grounded a twenty-two million dollar high tech flying machine.

Government Cow Shooter

May 1, 1980

It was raining last Friday, and like a lot of other loafers, I was sitting in Loretta's Cafe drinking coffee and listening to the gossip. My attention centered on Lonnie Morrison when I overheard him tell someone he once had a job shooting cows for the government. Sure enough! At one time, the US government hired cow-shooters.

Back in 1933 when the economy of the country was in a state called depression, Congress passed an act named the Agriculture Adjustment Act (AAA). The idea of the act was to control farm production. Henry A. Wallace was secretary of agriculture, and in 1934, he came up with the perfectly logical plan that the way to control livestock production was to do away with some of the cows and sows. So that's what they did. They bought the cows for something less than ten dollars a head and then they shot them.

One of the collection places for these cattle was a big pasture on the Canadian River north of Cantonment. The farmers and stockmen brought their animals in on Monday through Thursday and collected a receipt from the government agent which was negotiable at the banks. Friday was killing day.

It was a pretty economical plan as government plans go. Mr. Wallace's economic advisors had pointed out how the government could save money by not butchering and processing the animals into roasts and hamburgers. So they shot the cows and let them lay for the scavengers.

At that time, there was about a 32 percent unemployment rate among the white people and about a 93 percent unemployment rate among the Indians. There was no shortage of scavengers in the pasture near Cantonment.

The shooting was a cheap operation too. They paid two cents a head.

"I furnished my own saddle horse and rifle and the government furnished the cartridges. It seemed like good pay to me. I'd been working for two-bits a day plus room and board," Lonnie said.

The Deer Slayer

> *Fairview Republican (AP) The Six Million Dollar Man has been accused of killing a deer out of season, during the Grand National Quail Hunt.*
>
> —*Tahoe Daily Tribune* (Nevada) November 28, 1980

It saddened me a little to read in the Enid paper yesterday that the California deer slayer got a change of venue, and, now, all of the legal business concerning the above ruckus has been moved to the Woods County Courthouse in Alva.

I tell you, Fairview and Major County were getting a lot of publicity out of that affair, and, now, it turns out we weren't even entitled to it. The deer and the hunter were two miles too far north last month when they had that unfortunate meeting. Nobody involved in the thing was even in Major County.

That's the way things go sometimes. Too bad for Alva and Woods County. Maybe they can get some national coverage too at the upcoming hearing. I doubt that the hearing will amount to much. It is getting to be a kind of dull story. We got the cream of the publicity.

There for a while it looked like the poor deer that got shot one day too early was going to become as famous as Rudolph the Red Nose.

He was certainly the most famous deer that ever got shot *almost* in Major County.

Dog Tale

December 8, 1983

There has been a brown dog hanging around this place for quite a long time. When he first showed up here, he was lean and lank and had a full set of sound teeth. Now he has a middle-aged thickness and a careful way of moving that makes him appear more powerful than he really is. His upper lip on the right side is paralyzed and is usually hung-up on top of his one remaining fang. This gives him snarlish sneer which is pathetic.

After he arrived here, I hoped for a long time that someone would show up to claim him. No one ever did. He finally became the children's pet. He has had free run of the place now for nine years, and he has had only three rules to follow: Don't chase the cattle, don't eat the cat, and don't come in the house.

Well, there are other rules too, such as don't dig up the flowers, but he never caught on to that one.

As a farm dog, he has earned his living by keeping away the unwanted dogs that town folks kick out in front of farm homes. Except the females, of course. He always invites them in.

He knows the fields we farm and he goes to them and comes home as he will. Or he did up until a couple of years ago. Now he wants to ride in the back of the pickup. If we go off and leave him in some field, he just waits there until somebody comes back to get him.

It irks me when that happens, and sometimes I just leave him there until next day.

In the years that he has been here, he has never been anything but a nice dog to anyone who will give him a soft word and a pat on the head. As a watch dog, he is a total failure. He is quiet when cars drive in and barks like the devil when they drive out.

His fearlessness with other animals is far greater than his judgment. He has tangled with coyotes, badgers, skunks, and other dogs that outweighed him by fifty pounds. He has been stitched up and laid up many times but he never learned anything from the experiences. He is not very intelligent.

Last week, we lost him. He was gone for a day and a half before we missed him, which shows you that I am not sentimental about this beast. I take him for granted. He is always around here somewhere.

It seemed obvious that he had gotten out of the pickup at some stop I had made the day before. I started looking for him.

Three days later, Wilma Baird called me at five thirty in the morning from Love's Country Store. "Your dog is sitting out here in front of the door," she said.

When he got into the pickup, I scolded him for not being there yesterday or the day before that when I came back to pick him up. He just grunted.

Then I noticed the heavy chain collar fastened around his neck. He had never had a collar in his life. Where he got it, I will never know, and it doesn't make any difference. I picked him up where he got out of the pickup, which is the way we have been doing it now for a couple of years.

I invited him to sleep in the house that night. He was a perfect guest. No fuss, no mess, no noise. I am thinking about making it a permanent arrangement.

Draft Horses

February 14, 1980

Maybe now is the time to get into the draft horse business. Draft horses are coming back. A new day is dawning for work horses. Any kind is good: Percheron, Clydesdale, Belgian, Suffolk, or Shire. A good team of any breed will fetch a high price today.

If that sounds a little wild to you, consider these tidbits of information gleaned from the February issue of *Smithsonian* magazine:

In the peak year of 1937, 3,196 Belgian foals were registered. The 1980 registration is expected to exceed that. The total registration in 1952 was 171 foals.

At the Waverly Midwest Horse Sale held last October in Waverly, Iowa, 387 work horses and sixteen mules sold at auction for $672,595. That figures to an average price of $1,669 per head.

Worried about a harness? No sweat. There is an Amish man in Author, Illinois who will build you a stout set with chrome hames for 1500 bucks.

Well, a couple of years ago, I bought a brand new tractor with all the stuff on it the salesman could think of, and I can't see right now where draft horses are ever going to be any big thing in my life.

Back in the thirties, my uncle was still hanging onto one last team, old Babe and Bill. I do not recall them with any nostalgia or love.

I was the chore boy, their attendant as it were. They ate an awful lot of oats and hay. They had to be curried every single day. I stood on a wobbly stool to drag the harness up on them. And they were hard-mouthed.

Despite all that, a young man might today find the draft horse business both novel and profitable.

Fish Story

November 13, 1980

I guarantee this story is almost 100 percent true because I checked it out with Raymond Keeton.

It is as natural for a fisherman to lie as it is for a cat to land on its feet. The most wonderful lies of all are those lies told by one fisherman to another fisherman. The more expert the fishermen are, the more fanciful the lies are.

Here is one that was pulled off with no words exchanged (if you can believe that).

Bill Jordan, Fairview's retired police force, and his fishing buddy Russell Lovely were returning home from the river early in the evening after a good day's fishing. Their car trunk was loaded with big catfish.

Heavy rains had fallen the week before. Here and there, the roadside ditches were full of water. A perfect setup for a little more fun (only an expert could come up with one like this).

Mr. Jordan and Mr. Lovely parked the car by the side of the road and rigged out their fishing rods. They each tied a big catfish to the line and tossed the fish into the ditch of water. Then they sat down and waited for passersby. Whenever a car approached, they hauled out the fish and let them flop around on the roadside. Cars slowed down. Sometimes they stopped. The fishermen stuck to their business, silently hauling big fish out of the ditch. People gawked and drove on, amazed.

Tiring of the sport, the pranksters packed up and went happily home, congratulating each other for another fine successful day.

The best part of this grand lie was yet to come.

Next day dawned perfect weather for fishing. Our fishermen headed back to the river for another day with the catfish. All along the ditch where they had pulled their stunt the evening before, they found the road lined with parked cars and would-be fishermen squatting patiently by the water's edge waiting for the big cats to bite.

Fishing Problems

Mac and Augie cleaning fish

August 13, 1981

Canton Lake was formed forty years ago by what was then called the longest earthen dam in the world. According to the US Corps of Engineers who built it, one of the primary reasons for its construction was to furnish irrigation water to farmers.

As far as I know, the only irrigation water coming out of Canton Lake is sprinkled on lawns and gardens in Oklahoma City. When the lake gets full or Oklahoma City needs more water, the big gates in the dam are opened and the water moves down the Canadian River to the Oklahoma City reservoir.

It has been a drought year and the lake is low. The water has, in places, receded a couple hundred yards from the normal shoreline and along the rocks of the dam the water is way, way down.

This has created a distressing problem for one of our local fishermen.

Ray Keeton has fished Canton Lake since, well, for a long, long time. Like all experienced fishermen, he has favored places to fish from—certain rocks on the dam—certain logs and tree stumps along the shore. The problem is, with the water so low now, he has an awful time casting to it. He is wearing out his lines and reels and getting permanent cramps in his arm and shoulder.

And that's not the only nuisance to it, Ray says. When he is fortunate enough to hook, say, a two-pound fish, by the time he drags it in over all that sand and rocks the sucker is worn down to half a pound!

Clearly, a problem with no solution.

Food and Fitness

October 20, 1983

At the north edge of town, there is an establishment named the Fitness Factory. It is an exercise salon, a gymnasium for ladies dissatisfied with the shape of things. It is for the young and old, the fat and thin, and the healthy and the ailing.

I would like to attend one of their sessions, but I never shall. They won't let me in. It is only for ladies. It is for ladies who prefer to do their calisthenics behind closed doors in the company of like-minded ladies.

My wife announced some weeks ago she had signed up for a three month go-around with the fitness folks. When I asked why, she told me she was no longer a spring chicken and believed she was sagging and drooping and getting round in all the wrong places. She also thought it would tone her muscles, stimulate her blood, and possibly improve her mind. She made it sound like a bargain.

I figured I was in for another one of those diet programs where the refrigerator fills up with cottage cheese and lettuce and the bread drawer runs over with saltless crackers and airy wafers.

I can't tell you much about what goes on at the Fitness Factory except that it sounds strenuous. They have mechanical contrivances there that are designed to roll out the lumps and smooth in the hollows. A kind of land-leveling machine for use on the human body.

The costume they wear during these sessions is interesting and useful: long-sleeved purple leotards. It is useful because it causes the wearer to perspire profusely. They sweat a lot and the surplus pounds just drip on the carpet. The leotards are useful in another way. They readily reveal the lumps that need leveling.

I don't know if my wife has got herself shaped up to her satisfaction or not. She talks about lost inches but she does not dwell on lost pounds. She does seem to be more agile and stronger. She doesn't groan as much as she used to when I ask her out to help me lift something I can't manage myself.

I think the biggest improvement the Fitness Factory has wrought in our lives is the quantity and quality of the meals around here. I tell you, we are eating high on the hog. All that exercise and those sessions in the sauna have stimulated her appetite to a high pitch. We are having a lot of roast beef and apple pie lunches, and it is steak and chocolate cake almost every evening.

Food and Movies

January 17, 1980

We went over to Enid a few nights ago with the married kid and spouse to eat Chinese food and see a movie.

We ordered a fish dish, a pork dish, a beef dish and a poultry dish. It was tasty and plentiful enough but I have come to one conclusion: the Chinese places operate just like the pizza places and the Mexican places.

They offer you a multitude of dishes. Then they lather each dish with their one basic sauce. Same goes for the barbeque business. A good sauce could make de-boned sparrows tasty.

After some discussion we went to see the movie. Black Hole—a science fiction thing that runs pretty much like an updated John Wayne movie.

Lots of shootouts, characters with southern accents (robots), no kissing, and the good guys win.

A very nice evening.

I still prefer thick steaks and movies like *Butch Cassidy and the Sundance Kid*.

Give the Ball to Emri

I was fumbling through a box of old school junk one evening when I came upon the picture of Emri Heady dressed in his football gear. I was really looking for a strange certificate I got one time. It endowed me with the title: "Champion, Marbles, Fifth Grade."

It's an official looking certificate as a government bond, a scrolly thing, with signatures and stamps and all that. I can hardly believe it even when I'm looking at it. In those days, by George, they knew how to honor real talent. At any rate, I came across Emri's picture and it came to me why I don't care a thing about watching football games. Not in the stands, and not on the tube. It is not a spectator sport. It's a participation sport. And since I am long past that kind of action, the thing is all dead to me. The word "football" is, in fact, just another info-bit in the computer of my mind.

And this is how it goes: Say the word football, read the word, hear the word, glimpse a picture on the tube. Whatever. The gears and lights, the electricity and switches of my mind do all their instant things. And the cells of memory flash to my inner vision an image of the slight, frail, tight-wired Emri on a seventy-yard run, alone, through an army of wicked giants. He was, no question about it, the greatest open field runner of all time. Broken field runner, I think we called it then. From Granger to Namath, none have excelled him.

We played back in the days when the quarterback was the general of the action. The coach just watched, and from time to time, sent in the substitutes. He sent in his hopes. They seldom came with information.

In practice, he worked us to the point of total exhaustion and that's a long and rigorous sweat for seventeen- to eighteen-year-old farm boys.

Then we had skull practice, the memorizing of plays elaborately diagramed on a blackboard. He was strong for this business and throughout the school day, kept us alert all the time. he might, for instance, in the middle of demonstrating a theorem in geometry, stop and say, "Jackson, what do you do on play six?"

Then, he also held private tutoring sessions for the quarterbacks. Both of them. He instructed this year's general and he readied next year's general. We had some great ones. There was Jackson and Harp and Stafford and others too.

When the coach sent Emri in, anybody could have been the quarterback. And we all knew it because no matter what play was called, 15X or Statue of Liberty, the gist of the plan was, "Give the ball to Emri."

In those days, seven or eight of us always played the full time, both offense and defense. It was strenuous. With Emri, it was different.

After four or five runs, the coach pulled him out. He usually scored at least once, sometimes twice and in one blazing five minutes, he scored three times. That time, they carried him off the field like a wet towel.

It used to irritate me immensely when the coach pulled him. "Leave him in," I would growl to myself, "and we can beat the clowns by a hundred points."

The coach, Robinson was his name—was—of course, much wiser than that. Emri wasn't the big gun. He was the secret

35

weapon. We had lots of big guns, but only one Emri. He came in when we *had* to score. The rest of us scored too, from time to time. After all, Old Roby used to say at every skull practice, "Every play is a touchdown play if you all do the right thing."

I was always considerably guilt ridden in those times because in the heat of the onslaught, things seldom went exactly according to the plan of the play. When Emri came in, nothing went according to plan. We started with a plan, a play, a skull-practice-blackboard image, but in the end, he always did it on his own.

He often went gazelling across the goal line on the north side of the field while his interference phalanx galloped resolutely down the south side.

In practice scrimmage sessions, the coach was always chewing on Emri. He didn't follow the plan. Poor Emri. In the game, though, when we got down to the nitty-gritty, here came Emri.

He weighed about 140 pounds after a good solid meal. He was small, lithe muscled, tight nerved, quiet, even aloof. He was very fast. He was dynamite and the ball was his fuse. He exploded when it touched him. Not with blunt power, but with speed and agility. He called up his total energy and went flitting down the gridiron like a swallow catching mosquitoes in a stubble field. "Rabbit," we wanted to call him, but he didn't care for that.

Sometimes they nailed him. It was like bricks falling on a match stick house. Usually, it was somebody else's fault. A bad pass from center. A fumbled hand-off. What? Then they bombed him.

When that happened, the coach and the waterboy would drag him back to the bench and Band-Aid him back together. If the damage was serious, Dr. Johnson would be called in from the field with his satchel full of splints and tapes and little jars of real fine pills.

Dr. Johnson was the ultimate in super football nuts. He was the number one fan at all games. Home and abroad into the foreign towns of northwest Oklahoma. He was always there. But that is another story and we were talking about Emri, the football player. In such a crisis, he would limp and stagger out to take the ball again and do his absolute, complete damnest.

The spectacularity of his total output, his running, has never been equaled. Just to have passed him the ball: *Man ! That was football!*

Fortunate Mistake

One of the more exciting things about Christmas occurs after December 25. It can go on for days, perhaps even weeks. It involves going back to stores to exchange gifts of clothing for the proper size and color. This necessitates the planning of trips downtown, over to Enid and maybe to Oklahoma City. I heard of one lady who is going to Dallas soon to exchange a coat.

My wife was not very lucky this year. She didn't get to return anything. I bought her a two-piece dress downtown that was of faultless style and color and turned out to be a perfect fit.

I naturally accepted her expressions of appreciation and the kind comments of my daughters with graciousness and modesty.

I can now confess that it came about by accident—by a saleslady's mistake.

After everyone agreed the dress was perfectly correct in every way, some snoopy kid discovered the blouse was marked one size and the skirt another. Yet it was a perfect fit. Up until that moment, I did not know that my wife required one size at the top side and a different size on the bottom end.

Nevertheless, I lied and told my family I had ordered it that way.

Benjamin Franklin Likes Turkey

When the eagle was selected for our nation's symbol, Benjamin Franklin objected.

Ben thought we ought to use the wild turkey. It was a beautiful and useful bird, he argued. It was a common bird and flourished everywhere. He pointed out that the turkey was edible, whereas the eagle was not. Ben Franklin lived into his eighties and he served this country well. He was a super patriot.

Had he lived to be 120 and kept all his faculties he would have favored the mosquito as our nation's symbol.

The mosquito had done us more good than all the eagles and turkeys that ever flew or skittered across this land. The United States would not even exist today if it were not for the mosquito.

When the English general, Cornwallis, surrendered to George Washington in the swamps of Yorktown on October 19, 1781, he surrendered because one-fourth of the army was abed with malaria, a disease spread by mosquitoes.

Cornwallis was the best general the British had. He was in a fortified position. Thirty-five ships waited him offshore with troops and material. He could have stomped Washington's feet into the swamp.

The mosquito beat him. He gave up.

Another time, in 1802, Napoleon controlled all the land of the Mississippi watershed. It extends from New Orleans up that mighty river through fourteen states. Napoleon thought he was fighting in Haiti. He was not. He was fighting mosquitoes.

He gave up. He sold the Louisiana Purchase to Tom Jefferson for fifteen million dollars. He had lost 40,000 soldiers to the mosquito.

I live in the Mississippi watershed. I make my living here. I think Tom Jefferson and the mosquito did a good thing.

Frog Story

January 1, 1981

Practical jokes never amount to much unless you get some cooperation from the victim. If the fellow gets mad or upset, the whole thing just becomes an embarrassment to everybody.

Here is a little one that turned out pretty good.

Characters: The Victim, Junior Garman; the Jokers, Bill Jordan and Ray Keeton. Scene: Fishing, Canadian River.

After a slow, dull morning Ray and Bill returned to the pickup for noon lunch. They had caught nothing except a giant bullfrog.

While they waited for Junior to come in, they emptied his lunch box. It was one of those heavy duty boxes with a place built into the lid for a thermos bottle. They took out the sandwiches, crammed the struggling frog down into the box, and snapped the lid shut.

It was a chilly day. When Junior finally showed up for lunch, they decided to sit in the pickup. They maneuvered Junior into the middle.

If you don't know Junior, I have to tell you he is good natured and just a mite skittish. He startles easily. In fact, he is goosey.

So, he opened the box and let out a scream. Naturally, the bullfrog croaked, hunched its shoulders, bunched its legs, and prepared to escape. Junior slammed the lid shut—on his thumb. He screamed again. This time, in pain.

He turned pale, clenched his jaws, and stared straight ahead.

Bill and Ray quieted their laughter. They became concerned. Was he badly hurt? Was it still a joke?

With his hand on the lid and his thumb still caught, Junior soberly looked first at one joker and then the other.

Quietly, he said to them, "It don't take me long to look at a bullfrog."

Hubert

One of the difficult things about farming is that every once in a while, you have to get devious and deceitful with your own family.

I made the mistake one morning of referring to the breakfast bacon as "Hubert's left flank." Hubert was some child's 4-H project who, after the shows was over, metamorphosed into bacon and hams.

It was a terrible mistake. The children left the table. My wife made bad puns, telling me, along with other things, that it was certainly a tasteless remark.

Another time, we had a gaggle of geese. They are interesting creatures and useful too. For one thing, they killed out all the sandburs and goatheads for a quarter mile around the farmstead.

Basically though, they are a nuisance. They messed up the cattle's water tank, intimidated the cat and dog, nibbled the bark off young trees, and were forever wandering through the workshop.

One morning, I decided to butcher them. Everybody likes roast goose. I slaughtered a couple of them and called for help with the feathers and so on. Nobody came. In fact, nobody was home. While I was out killing geese, everybody else remembered urgent business in town.

After dressing two geese by myself, I stuck them in the freezer and left home too.

I went out west of town to see a friend who has a great big pond down in a cedar canyon. I convinced him that what he needed on that pond were some white geese. I pointed out how pleasant it would be to stroll down to his pond at sunset to watch the geese at play.

He took them.

It didn't work though. Within two weeks coyotes ate the geese.

Gold

January 24, 1980

Well, the price of gold keeps going up. It hit $800 an ounce this week. I pointed out to my wife that these thirty dollar wedding bands we put on about a hundred years ago are probably worth a lot of money on the gold market. She pointed out that I am probably wrong because her ring has worn mighty thin.

Remember when you could treat a friend to a cup of coffee and have one too for a thin silver dime?

With thin silver dimes selling for a buck and a half nowadays, a cup of coffee for two bits is a sure enough bargain.

And a genuine silver dollar today for one bushel of wheat would make wheat farmers obscenely rich indeed. How in the world do you know when you are well off?

Grapes and Winemaking

April 9, 1981

One of my great-grandfathers emigrated from a wine producing region in Europe. He settled in Missouri where he raised grapes, horses, and a host of children.

One of his children, my great-uncle Fred Kreutz, came to Oklahoma when the Cherokee Strip opened. He homesteaded three miles north of Fairview where he soon decided he had made a mistake. His grapes would not grow.

Uncle Fred moved down to the Chickasha area where he got a farm that would grow grapes. He turned the grapes into wine which he sold by the barrel. In that way he made his honest living until January 29, 1919 when the 18th Amendment to the US Constitution went into effect. The 18th Amendment prohibited citizens of the US from making, transporting, or selling wine.

Since his family had been grape growers and wine makers for countless generations, Uncle Fred never fully understood what the 18th Amendment was all about.

For some time, he kept right on doing what he had always done. By then though, it was a dishonest, illegal, and disreputable business. When his family and the local sheriff and the Internal Revenue agents finally made that all very clear to him, he quit.

He went into the grape jelly business. It was a half-hearted attempt to adjust to the changing times. He sold grape juice by the barrel and handed each customer a recipe for grape jelly. He also told each customer how to salvage the juice in case it started fermenting before they turned it into jelly.

It was, for my great-uncle, a dismal way to make a living.

In the first place, there were not many people equipped to make a barrel of jelly. In fact, there were not many people who even wanted a barrel of jelly. The folks who bought the juice and attempted to make their own wine were soon discouraged by the same forces that stopped Uncle Fred.

Uncle Fred is long gone and so is his vineyard. The field where it flourished has been raising wheat and cattle for half a century now.

I got to thinking about that ancient uncle and his vineyard after reading an article in the May issue of *Quest* magazine. The article describes what must surely be the most valuable piece of farmland in all the world.

It is, of course, a vineyard. A small vineyard of four and one-half acres. The boundaries of which have not changed in 250 years. In a countryside crowded with the best vineyards in the world, this one small plot is considered the very best.

It has been sold only four times since the sixteenth century. Each time it brought a fabulous price. It is today valued at twenty million dollars and it is not for sale.

Part of this tremendous value might be because of the vineyard's fame and antiquity—but not necessarily. The wine from a single year's production sells for over a million dollars.

That is a five percent return on the land's value and quite a bit more than a certain Major County wheat field will return this year.

Hard Gridirons

At Durant, school official plan to drill a well to irrigate the football practice field. School officials say that, without water soon, the field would be so hard it would be unsafe to play on.

—The Sunday Oklahoman August 24, 1980

By George, I wish some school officials in Canton, Waynoka, Okeene, Cherokee, Woodward, or Fairview had come up with that idea forty years ago.

All of those towns had bare hard gridirons as I remember them, except Waynoka. The Waynoka field was soft. The north end of it was blow sand, and the south end was cushioned with a healthy crop of Texas goatheads.

Somewhere, we played on a field that was topped with cinders (mixed with some fair sized clinkers) that had been hauled in from the nearby railroad yard. The cinder topping was a fine way to firm up the blow sand but it didn't do much to keep down sand burrs and goatheads. It was a great surface for running on, but oh boy, when you hit the deck everything smarted.

One of our boy's hands got so torn up and punctured with burrs he went into the second half of the game wearing leather gloves borrowed from the bus driver.

It was just another good idea that didn't work.

The game officials made him take them off. "Too dangerous," they told him. "You could be concealing a rock or a chunk of lead in those gloves. You might hurt somebody. Gloves are not allowed."

I'm not one to dwell on the old days. I hope Durant and every other town with a football field has an ample supply of water and fertilizer so they can keep their turf thick and soft.

High Adventure

Fifty years ago this month, a half-blind Oklahoma farm boy and oil field worker climbed into a small single engine airplane and headed out across the Atlantic Ocean. He flew around the world. Four days and some hours later, he landed back where he began.

In that single flight, Wiley Post in the "Winnie Mae" broke so many flying records and established so many firsts that his name will stand forever in the annals of aviation history.

In the heart and mind of every human being, lurks the desire to do something no other person has ever done. Most of us never get around to even attempting satisfying such desires and the world is probably a safer and saner place because we don't.

Parents spend a lot of time restraining children from dangerous and ill-conceived projects while common sense controls most adults from carrying out rash ideas.

Common sense, however, does not always win out.

One afternoon twenty-odd years ago, while fishing near the Red Banks on the south side of Canton Lake, a friend of mine decided to do something no one else had ever done. He decided to sail across the lake. I said that a lot of people had sailed across Canton Lake by then so there was nothing unique about that idea.

"It is not what you do that counts," he said. "It is how you do it that is important. I will sail across the lake on an inner tube in the middle of a moonless night and tonight is the night."

Once I understood that he would not be swayed from this ambitious plan, I asked the obvious question. "How will you fix a sail and a rudder to an inner tube?"

He assured me that there was nothing to it. He had been reading up on sailing vessels in the encyclopedia. "I can rig it up in thirty minutes," he said. "Meet me here at ten o'clock tonight. I will need a witness."

"I am not going with you."

"Certainly not, this is a solo voyage. All you do is see me off then drive your pick up around and meet me on that sandy cove near the north end of the dam. With this breeze, I can cross in two hours."

At 11:00 p.m., he shoved off sitting on a sheet of plywood wired to a tractor inner tube. Some kind of two-by-four arrangement held up the sail.

"Sail ho!" he shouted and disappeared into the night.

Four hours later, he waded ashore at the meeting place. Shortly after I had left him, the wind died. He had swum across the lake towing his contraption behind him.

"Help me load this thing. I have to get this tube back on the tractor; my brother wants to plow today."

On the way home, he swore me to secrecy. "There is nothing more humiliating and embarrassing than a daring feat gone badly," he said. He was glum.

I tried to cheer him by telling him he was no doubt the first person to swim across Canton Lake towing a sailing vessel. He saw no glory in that.

We talked about this adventure a couple weeks ago. He wants to remain anonymous.

Hound Dogs

December 20, 1979

I see in the public records at the courthouse where the Fairview State Bank is mortgaging coon hounds.

When I first read this, I naturally wondered how much I could borrow on Old Rex. He has not had much experience with coons, but he is a holy terror to stray cats.

Also noticed where a fellow mortgaged his cook stove, his bedroom furniture, and his electric golf cart.

That fellow has my sympathy. When a man can't eat, bed, or golf without worrying about some rascal foreclosing on his equipment, you know he has got to be a nervous, restless candidate for stomach ulcers.

Somehow or another, thinking about the plight of that poor chap reminds me of the tranquil days I spent in the military service: Free board and room, an abundance of wholesome exercise, and pocket money for beer and cookies. Not a care in the world.

Enough of that. I'm spending the rest of the afternoon getting Rex interested in coons. I think it would be real satisfying to know I own a mortageable dog.

Isabella Auction

November 3, 1983

Last Saturday evening, the Isabella Hardware closed its doors on an empty shell. Bryan Patzkowsky has retired.

With three auctioneers crying the sale, changing off from time to time, the chanting went on for six solid hours. They stripped the store out from wall to wall, top to bottom, and front door to back door.

They sold it all, including the signs on the walls and a stack of leftover 1974 calendars which went for a buck.

They sold brand new things and old things. They sold digital watches and cream-separator oil. They sold kitchen mixers and new parts for old M&M tractors. They sold flashlights and rivets, nuts and bolts, and a stand-up desk. And a thing-a-majig that dispenses needles for 195 different makes of sewing machines.

It was a whale of a sale and the place was packed from start to finish.

Auctions fascinate me. A Major County auction is better than a stage play. It's better than a movie. It's better than Shakespeare on TV. It beats a football game hands down.

A good auctioneer is like a good actor. He entertains. He is a working psychologist. He holds the crowd. He offers bargains, treasures, things you suddenly need. He knows a little something about every kind of merchandise. He puts a good name on everything.

In the hullabaloo, he stays cool and on top of the chaos. He is there for one reason: exchange the goods for cash today. He never quits counting or analyzing the mob.

The only way I made it through the afternoon's boiling activity was to elbow my way over to the corner every hour or so to where the Mennonite ladies were handing out pie and coffee. That was the bargain of the day.

People at auctions do strange and mysterious things. They suddenly discover needs they never knew they had.

Why does my wife need a supply of needles for 195 brands of sewing machines? Why do I need another scoop shovel? We will never wear out the ones we have. What is Ike Neufeld going to do with fifteen potato peelers? Who needs twelve garlic squeezers or a stack of 1974 calendars? Why did that little old lady buy a double-bit ax? Tough questions.

According to Bill Wright, the hardware store auction was Isabella's biggest day. According to my cousin Bob, Isabella's biggest day was the day he was born there in the post office.

But that's another story. You could ask Aunt Emma about it. She knows all the details.

Jug Run

Model T topped off

June 1980

In the late 1920s, a little group of townsmen met occasionally for recreation in the backroom of Doc Johnson's drug store. The name of their game was *Straight Pitch*. It may be that they gambled. I don't know, and anyway, that's not what this story is about.

Sometimes, a jug of booze was brought to the game and from time to time, throughout the evening, the jug was passed around the table. Some players nipped and others did not. Some thought it improved the game. Others knew better.

On one such evening, the jug ran dry early in the game. Not real early. It ran dry just as things were going good. The local bootlegger was called upon for relief. No luck.

He was sold out.

One of the more widely traveled of the gentlemen spoke up. "There is a bootlegger in Carmen who never runs out. Let's run up to Carmen."

No good. The river bridge on the road between Orienta and Cleo had washed out the night before.

It was then that a railroader in the group suggested a solution. They borrowed a locomotive and a coal tender from the railroad shop on the south side of town (the roundhouse). They eased it through town and then steamed on up to Carmen where they bought a full jug.

On the way back to Fairview, it occurred to someone that perhaps the locomotive would by now have been missed from the roundhouse. Some inquisitive Santa Fe official might be waiting for them.

They stopped two miles north of town and decided the prudent thing to do would be to abandon further rail transportation.

And that is what they did.

That is the end of the story, except to mention that next day, several Santa Fe Railroad detectives wandered around town asking intelligent questions for which no one had anything but stupid or smart aleck answers.

Keep on Trying to Learn

July 10, 1980

Somewhere along the line in my early youth, I picked up the idea that a person ought to keep trying to learn things throughout his life. Keep reading, ask questions, be inquisitive, listen, watch, absorb, analyze. You know what I'm talking about. Your mother or grandfather or some teacher probably told you the same thing.

I'm having second thoughts about the whole idea. I may give it up altogether. It's getting too confusing. Some of the things I inquire into are downright baffling.

For instance, I subscribe to a newspaper named *Kiowa County Press*. It is a weekly published in Eads, Colorado, population about nine hundred if everybody is home. It is a small paper, and what they see fit to publish in Kiowa County can be read in about twelve minutes and that includes all the ads and legal notices.

For some weeks now, I have noticed a small classified AD that reads, "Want to buy wheat, will pay with pre-1965 silver coins."

So I called his number a couple of nights ago and visited with a chap who seemed absolutely sincere in his desire to lay out silver coin for the golden grain.

He was quite open with his proposition and spoke with a good deal of assurance that everything would work just like he said it would. And two times, he cautioned me not to make decisions without consulting my income tax person. The actual amount of coin he will give for a specific amount of wheat hangs on the daily fluctuation of both the silver and wheat market, plus some specialty angles in the silver coin market. Big lots of silver coins come either bagged or rolled. They may be worked or slick.

I didn't know that. Did you know that?

Anyway, I finally asked him the nitty-gritty question. "If I take one thousand bushels into Sooner Co-op tomorrow morning and put it down to your name, what will be the face value of the silver coins you give me?"

"Let me hit the computer here," he said. In a moment he reported," It reads .18410 and I would round to 185. The face value of the coins would count to $185."

Is that a good deal? Eighteen-and-a-half cents a bushel for wheat. In 1965, we sold wheat for around $1.50 a bushel for the same kind of money—US silver coin. And things looked bleak then!

It certainly is a puzzle. A bafflement. Inquisitiveness certainly doesn't always bring contentment. I may give up trying to learn things.

Ladies in High Heels

For some time now, I've been aware that I don't always recognize some of the people I have known for years and years until I get up pretty near to them. I was about to decide that I probably have reached the bifocal stage of life. That I needed to go see Dr. Beavers and get measured for a set of prescription glasses. My TG&Y #22 spectacles just weren't filling the bill any longer.

I was crossing the street the other day when a lady in high heels stopped to wave at me. As I drew nearer, I saw it was my wife.

Eureka! I said to myself, it's not my eyes. It's those high fashion high heeled shoes that are throwing me off. Those shoes are pitching ladies into a different stance, a different way of walking, a different way of moving. No wonder I don't recognize some people until I can see the whites of their eyes.

It's a fact that on the street and in stores, we first recognize people we know by the way they move. Well, I think it is a fact.

Anyway, it seems obvious to me that ladies in high heels look and walk differently than they do in flat heels.

Walking in high heels necessitates a shifting body weight so as to lower the center of gravity. It also calls for a more highly tuned sense of balance. If you meet a lady in high heels with a look of concentration on her face, she is likely concentrating on her balance.

Walking is a process of balancing the entire body on one heel, and then falling forward (or backward or sideward) to another position and balancing the weight on the other heel. A lady stilted up on heels that are three-quarters of an inch square has a lot more to think about than a lady in sneakers.

Women handle the situation in four different ways: (1) a forward shift of the upper torso, (2) a backward shift of the lower torso, (3) the bent knee stride, (4) the stand-tall-take-short-steps method.

That's about as far as I want to carry this thing. I may be in for trouble the way it is.

I just think ladies in high heels look great and I think other men think so too, and I suppose that is why the ladies wear them.

Lawn Mowers

August 2, 1984

> *Total man-hours spent mowing lawns in the United States each year: 2,254,000,000.*
>
> —*Harper's Magazine* June 1984

Lawn mowing is a symbol of our affluence, proof of the vast wealth in this country. The total man-hours spent mowing lawns are thirty-five times more than all the man hours spent producing the yearly wheat crop. The time spent mowing is equal to 1,100,000 full time jobs every three days.

The amazing thing about all the work is most of it is done for no pay. It is just one of the chores we have all talked ourselves into doing. If one wants to put up a civilized appearance in the neighborhood, the lawn has to be mowed every week. To do the right and proper thing, the grass should be well fertilized and watered. Then it can be mowed every three days.

Everyone aspires to possess several thousand square feet of good Bermuda sod that grows nicely so that it can be clipped down to look like a fine green carpet.

This brings us to Edwin Budding.

In 1830, Edwin Budding, a foreman in an English carpet mill, was struck with a wonderful idea. He invented the lawn mower. It was a wonderful idea for Edwin, but I think it has turned out to be a laborious idea for the rest of us.

It is another example of how the invention of a labor-saving device created more work than anyone could have imagined. When Edwin Budding invented his wonderful machine, there were really very few people who knew they needed a lawn mower. People were content in their ignorance.

Before Budding's brilliant brainstorm, people who needed short clipped grass used sheep to do the work. Even today, on some golf courses in Scotland, sheep do the grass clipping. In Abe Lincoln's day, sheep and geese grazed the White House grounds.

"Necessity is the mother of invention." Not necessarily true. Budding invented the lawn mower, and the rest of the world, set to work and invented the lawn.

Actually, Edwin may not have been thinking much about lawns at all when the great idea struck him. He may have been further ahead of his time than that. He may have been thinking about an exercise machine.

"Country gentleman," he said, "will find in using my machine an amusing, useful, and healthful exercise."

Amusing? No.

Useful? Yes, if you want short grass and have no sheep.

Healthful? No, indeed! Lawn mowers are hazardous machines. They cut off fingers and toes and sometimes throw rocks. Sheep never do that.

Lice Racing

A good many people have heard this story in one version or another. A few will think they know from whom it originated. I put it down as a little bit of early-day history, exactly as it was told to me by an ex-Major County-ian. I say "ex-Major County-ian" because the man is dead. God rest his soul. I hope he is in heaven, but I wouldn't bet on it.

He was a tale teller. He could fix you with his pale blue eyes, and with an expressionless face, reel out a tall tale so convincingly, you couldn't help but believe it. He made you want to believe it. Even when your common sense told you it was all utterly ridiculous, you still wanted to believe it. He never even admitted by word or expression that any single word he spoke was anything less than the gospel truth. Maybe the tales he told were absolutely true. I really don't know.

Here is the Lice Racing story:

> My father homesteaded on a sandy, blackjack quarter, west of Longdale. When it came time for me to go to school, he sent me over to Old Cantonment, and I went to school with the Indian kids. We were just as poor as the Indian kids, and he figured it was where I would fit in best.
>
> The local Indians like racing horse racing, foot racing—any kind of racing. In Cantonment, we raced lice. Yeah, every kid that amounted to anything kept a trained louse for racing. We bet on races. We bet things like jackknives, sandwiches, balls of string, and marbles.
>
> I was tricking those poor Indian kids. I had two louses. A fast louse and a slow louse. I kept the slow louse behind my right ear. I'd use the slow louse for a while until the bets got real good. Then I'd slip in the fast louse.
>
> One day, I won Johnny Two Bull's moccasins and a beaded belt his grandma had made for him. Next day, Johnny's mama showed up at recess time.

She watched for a while as we squatted there in a circle, racing the lice. Finally, she reached down and pulled me up by the ear. "Ah, ha, Blue Eyes," she said, "Let me see them both." She put my two racers in the palm of her hand and looked at them. Then she picked out my fast louse and bit his head off.

It was a terrible loss to me. I think about it still.

Loretta's Cafe

January 10, 1980

Rainy weather puts a terrific burden on the waitresses at the local restaurants. Farmers shifting around from Loretta's Cafe to the Hiway Restaurant and on down to the Phillips 66 place keep the girls hopping and the coffee pots bubbling.

I am pretty sure there is no money made on coffee on a rainy day in Fairview. It takes three refills before guilt moves the loafers on down to the next cafe. Loretta's Cafe has probably got the best solution for everybody. She keeps lots of coffee pots going, has two quick-witted waitresses, gives no tickets, and there is a table by the exit where you make your own change and put down what you think you owe.

It is a system that would not work everywhere. That's one of the nice things about here.

Wheat farmers should not get panicky about the president's view on wheat trading and the international markets. It's a hail cloud and, as you know, most of them pass by.

A close analysis of the official statements lets you know that the Russians can buy our wheat today just like they could a month ago.

The only dumb thing about it is they pay for it with gold, and tomorrow, they will get more wheat for an ounce of gold than they got yesterday.

Mrs. Brown's Rooster

Anyone who has been around a wheat farm knows that most farmers get pretty nervous about spilled grain. Especially landlords checking out the renters at harvest time. My uncle almost died of apoplexy the first time I scooped off a load of wheat into his grain bin. I had missed the opening about a dozen times and had enough wheat on the ground to "feed a Chinaman for a year," he said.

I have heard a lot of stories about how frugal some folks are about spilled wheat, but none of them beats the one Gene Fast told me the other day.

Years ago, Mrs. Wally Brown owned a wheat farm east of town which she rented to Dan Fast and his sons. Mrs. Brown was a very conservative lady who paid close attention to her business. It was her custom to come out to the farm at harvest time to see that her share of the grain was properly accounted for and properly stored in her granary.

One afternoon, she looked over the situation around the granary door and concluded that an unnecessary and wasteful condition existed. Although the Fast boys had cleaned up all the spillage possible, there was still enough grain scattered in the dust and weeds to warrant salvaging.

Mrs. Brown went home to her chicken pen and returned to the granary with three Rhode Island Red roosters and a ball of twine. She tethered each rooster by one leg to the granary door and left for day, pleased, we can assume with her solution to this vexing problem. If anyone ever conceived of a more efficient way to salvage spilled grain, I never heard of it.

Unfortunately, like many plans worked out to the limits of efficiency, the plan backfired. A hungry skunk stopped by in the night and feasted on one of the roosters, leaving only two to peck the grain when the sun came up. In the middle of the hot day, one of the roosters simply settled down in the dust and gave up the ghost. Perhaps he died of gluttony, or heat exhaustion, or old age. No one knows.

Now, Mrs. Brown was a frugal woman, but she was not a foolish woman. That afternoon, when she saw what had happened, she cut her losses. She gathered up the one remaining rooster, rolled up the twine and went home.

If you want more details, see Gene Fast.

Mrs. Kent's Whistle

In all my forty-three years, the only person whose orders I've taken with eagerness and enthusiasm were those of Charlie Kent. Well, actually, he never gave orders. He merely stated what the modus operandi would be.

He was a leader for sure, and it's a good thing he went into the medical profession. I mean, it's a good thing for the world in general. It is probably a good thing he never went into politics or military maneuvers. If he had, the Misters Johnson, de Gaulle, Mao Tse, little-known Vito, Castro, and others of that ilk would, I'm sure, be unknown today.

Charlie was a kind of an Einstein-Genghis Khan super salesman type. On further reflection, it's rather a pity he didn't go into politics.

His ideas were unique and his plans superb. There was never the slightest doubt of his ultimate success—barring, of course, an act of God, or his mother's police whistle.

God and the Whistle stood on the same level and there wasn't anything to be done about either one except to alter the plan to fit the whims of God or the Whistle.

The only standing law of his life that I knew about was the Whistle. When the Whistle sounded, he went home. Immediately, from the top of a tree, or the bottom of a cave, he dog-trotted home. The Whistle called him in for meals and home for bed. As

I remember, it was the only absolute rule in his life. The rest of time and the universe was his cherry pie.

His imagination was flaming. For instance, he announced one afternoon in the middle of a marble game that it was time to go. We were ten and eleven years old and it was time to go.

So we left home.

We went leisurely and lightly packed. We carried a telescope, a canteen of water, a butcher knife, and some marbles. We traveled west.

Near sundown, we left the road to climb a butte. We were three miles from town. From the top of the butte, it looked a tremendous distance.

Squinting through the telescope, Charlie announced he could see his father leaving the ice plant office, getting into his Model A, going home for supper. Folding the telescope, Charlie changed our plan.

"We'll have to go back. She'll be blowing the Whistle."

It seemed perfectly logical to me. We walked steadily, and in an hour or so, we came to the edge of town, near the ice plant and the railroad tracks. It was dark. We could hear the whistle. A long blast, and about a minute later, another long blast. We broke into a dog trot down the middle of the street.

When we came to Charlie's house, he turned in. I slowed down to a walk. Right away, there was a lot of shouting and door slamming and barging around in Charlie's house. I walked the last block home.

My father was standing in the yard near the street light. I was ready for anything. When I came up to the driveway, he said from twenty to thirty feet away, "Go into the house. Your mother has supper ready."

It was fried chicken and gravy on cold biscuits. She seemed glad to see me. My sisters were in bed. I went to bed exhausted and relieved of punishment.

Charlie did not fare so well. His punishment was indeed severe. Confinement to his own yard for two days. He who ranged the town like a mongrel dog.

At the end of his second day of confinement, we had almost completed a tunnel under the garage which would lead a distance away from his yard to the public alley. There were, of course, easier ways to escape. He could have gone through the gate. No challenge to that though.

The next story I heard about Charlie was after the war and we were all GI billing our way through OU. A used-car dealer friend of mine in my hometown told me Charlie Kent had walked in about a year earlier and stated he had just gotten out of service and was on his way down to OU to study medicine (he hadn't yet at this time even gotten his high school diploma). What he needed most urgently was a sixty-five dollar car that would travel fifty miles a day for at least a year with no expense other than gasoline. With a kind of puzzled air, my friend told me he sold Charlie a car priced at $250 for $65 cash—small bills.

Charlie is a doctor, and I've seen him two times recently at the funerals of his parents, but I didn't get to talk to him much. He lives in Arizona, and I think when the wheat is sown this fall, I'll go out to visit with him.

Miss Schuh's Whistle

A big work crew for the Santa Fe spent one winter in our town laying a new track south to Altus. Among them was a Mexican family with many robust, sturdy children. They came to school one frosty morning and toward the end of the first recess I noticed them standing apart, watching the play around them. By way of introduction, I went up to them and said, "You are gypsies, aren't you?"

It was the wrong thing to say.

The biggest one stepped forward, put his chapped brown hand on my chest, gave me a mighty push, assumed a combative stand, and said, "I'm Spanish-American. If you call me gypsy, I'll fight you. I'll hit you in the nose till it bleeds. I might fight you right now."

This startled me. And the pushing enraged me. I too, became combative. We glared at each other, toe to toe. We sized each other. He looked heavier. He was heavier. He held his thumbs inside his fists. Twinges of fear tickled my back. He was surely a good fighter—with thumbs in his fists. He probably could make my nose bleed. Extra weight and strangely held fists are real facts to a fourth grader.

We were instantly ringed by half the school and my pal Kenny King didn't help when he shouted, "Hit him, Mac, and get the *scissor-holt* on him"

I had a reputation for my *scissor-holt*.

I was committed.

We would fight and I would get bloodied. I was sure I could never get the scissor-holt on him. He was too big around the middle. I was about to lose a lot of stature and get hurt to boot.

The terrible tenseness of that fearsome moment exploded with the call to class. Dear ol' sweet Miss Schuh and her beautiful police whistle. We couldn't start a fight with Miss Schuh right there calling us to line up for the march back to class. Everybody knew that. With sullen looks, we unclenched fists and to my vast relief moved away from each other.

I recalled that moment these thirty-odd years later and dredged up one other flash of thought that raced through my mind the very last instant of that toe-to-toe, fisted, eye-to-eye situation. Juan had a cold. His jaws were clenched. He was breathing hard. Every time he exhaled, a long globule of snot extruded down to his lip. When he inhaled, it drew back into his nose. My last thought was, hit him breathing in.

My Old Pickup

About fifteen years ago, I went to A. B. Kliewer's sale and bought his old pickup truck. It was a three-quarter ton job made by General Motors in 1959. The engine purred like a kitten full of sweet milk, and the bed was equipped with two sets of wood sideboards which A. B. had made himself.

I drove it home and figured I had a bargain. Even though it was nine years old, I knew it would serve me just fine for a couple of years, and by that time, I could surely afford a new one.

When I drove into my yard, I noticed the odometer read 29,999.9 miles. Which is exactly what it read when I left the sale. It needs a bit of oil, I thought. I will fix it in the morning. But I never did. It still reads 29,999.9.

During the fifteen years I have owned the pickup, it has been used hard. One could even say it has been abused. One child drove it to high school for three years. It sets outside winter and summer. We have worn out three sets of seat covers. The floor mat shredded out ten years ago and was replaced with a remnant of AstroTurf, which is holding up well. Its single taillight has been knocked off and replaced several times. Elfred Cornelsen overhauled the engine several years ago and it still runs great. It starts easier and quicker than any motor on this farm and goes just about anywhere a tractor will go.

The last time Ed Heffel welded the door hinges together he said, "I don't know how long that will last, but I do know we can't do it again." That was fourteen years ago.

If you think I have sentimental attachment to this pickup, you are wrong. I detest the thing. I am sick and tired of it. I don't need it. We have two much newer pickups. But somehow or another, every few days, some job comes up that we can only do with the old pickup.

Sometimes, it distresses me. I don't know what to do with it. I park it out of sight behind the barn. It's a real junker.

I can't trade it in because no dealer wants it. I sold it to a fellow who intended to restore it to its original condition, but when he started checking around for door hinges and such things, he backed out of the deal. At one time or another, I have offered to give it to every kid in the family. No way, papa.

A couple of years ago, I loaned it to Jake Boehs who took it to Colorado to spray weeds. When they drove away, I thought, ah ha, gone at last. It can stay in Colorado forever. Four months later, without even asking me, he loaded it on a grain truck and brought it back! Four hundred miles!

Right now, it is sitting in the shed with twenty bushels of leftover seed wheat in it. Tomorrow, I am going to take it to town and dump the wheat out of it. Then I guess I will park it out behind the barn. It might come in handy when we start building electric fences next fall.

PS: We have worn out several new pickups since I bought "Frog." One of the kids glued a green ceramic frog on the dash twenty years or so ago. Hence, the name "Frog."

Note: *This was sent into a farm magazine and Mac won a set of Goodyear Wrangler Radial tires, which he put on a much newer truck.*

Newspapers

The April 4 *Sunday Oklahoman* weighed three pounds. That figures out to two bits a pound for reading material, which isn't bad. Putting it that way makes it sound like I got more for my money than if I just said I paid seventy-five cents for a newspaper.

As it turned out, I didn't buy much newspaper. What I bought was mostly a catalog. That irked me. I figure catalogs ought to be free. I remember a day when catalogs were free and useful things of value even if you didn't want to read them. Those days, thank God, have passed. For me, catalogs are just a nuisance to be gotten rid of.

I realize that not everyone feels that way about catalogs or there wouldn't be so many of them printed. And my wife wouldn't keep a three foot stack of them in the hallway. But, back to the *Sunday Oklahoman.*

When I walked into the house with my three pounds of news, I bumped into the refrigerator and dropped the paper. It scattered all across the floor. In gathering it up, it came to me that I was picking up a lot of what they call "Newspaper Advertising Supplements." I counted them. There were twelve.

One of them, Montgomery Ward, contained six newspaper-sized pages. Hurrah for Montgomery Ward! They not only tricked me into carrying home their catalog, I paid somebody for the privilege.

I became intrigued. I folded all the supplements together and laid them on the kitchen scale. They weighed fifteen and one-half ounces. The classified AD section weighed seven ounces. The TV guide and the regular magazine supplement weighed nine ounces. The funnies weighed one ounce. The newspaper part of the newspaper, including the women's section, the sports section and the business pages weighed thirteen and one-half ounces. Some newspaper!

About this time, my wife came into the kitchen to fix breakfast. She was puzzled. "You are weighing the pages of the newspaper?" she asked. I explained to her the nature of my investigation. "Oh," she said, "let me see that Montgomery Ward thing. They have good sales this time of year."

I pulled out the funnies and handed her the whole blamed thing. Some days you can't get your point across no matter what you do.

One Man Won the Trophy

The death this week of Jesse Owens, the great star of the 1936 Olympics, reminded me of the "Cheyenne Clipper."

All athletes recall some day of blazing glory. If not their own, then someone else's they have known. It was a high school track meet in the spring of 1941. Fairview, Alva, Cherokee, Waynoka, and other schools in the area gathered in Woodward for a big meet.

We gathered by the busloads. Track was big in those days. Yes, except for the Cheyenne Clipper, the teams traveled in buses. He came from somewhere in Roger Mills County in a car with his coach. He was all the team they had. He was all they needed.

Late in the afternoon when it was all over, he, it was, that stepped up to take the team trophy. He had gathered more points than any busload there. He won five first places. I recall them vividly. He won the 100 yard dash, the 220, the 440, the half-mile run and the broad jump. He was built on the lines of Jim Thorpe, and he won easily and handily—one event after another.

He won, for instance, the half-mile run and without stopping, trotted over to the broad jump pit where he was next up. He waited a minute or so, breathing heavily, while they dusted the jump board and leveled the sand in the pit. Then he sailed out there nearly twenty-four feet. That was enough. He just jumped the one time.

I remember someone saying, "One day, he will out-do Owens." He never did. In fact, I never heard of him again. I am sorry to say I do not even remember his name, if I ever knew it. A rumor floated around the meet that warm afternoon. He was twenty years old and would be leaving for military service in a few weeks.

Someday, I plan to drive out to Roger Mills County and see if I can find someone who remembers the "Cheyenne Clipper."

Poignant Tale

August 20, 1981

Some time ago, a middle-aged lady told me a sweet, sad, maybe funny kind of story, and this is what she told me.

"I walked to a one-room school a mile away from our little farm and I loved school. On stormy days, my father took me in our old pickup and he would grumble about the nuisance of it.

I rode six miles to high school on a bus. To my father, it was a waste of time. He never pretended to understand that an A grade was better than a C grade or that algebra was anything more than a foolish game.

I went away to college without his blessing or a dime of his money. It took me five years to get through, and I worked every low-paying job you can imagine to pay my way.

When I got my degree in its red leather folder, I sent it home in a brown manila envelope to show him what I had accomplished. He sent it back by return mail and I stuck it in the bottom of my dresser drawer.

In all my trips home to visit in the years that followed, my father never asked me one question about my college days. The diploma in its folder was shifted and moved around like the other things we all keep but never look at.

Years after my father died, I opened the folder for no reason but to call up old memories. A small envelope fell out. It was a note from my father, "I am proud of you," it read. In with that short note were $100 bills—the most cash, I am sure, my father ever had his hands on."

Puns

A pun is a humorous play on words greatly enjoyed by children and simple-minded folks like myself. If you don't like puns, read no further.

Here is one I got last week from David Wahl in Isabella.

Once upon a time, a powerful chief lived in a great grass house in the heart of Africa. His tribe was happy and contented. The people lived in good grass houses, had plenty of food, and only went to war once in a while.

Every year, the tribe paid tribute to the chief. The tribesmen gave him lumps of gold. He finally had so much gold he didn't know what to do with it. So he built a golden throne which he kept in the attic of his house.

Every year, he added more gold to the throne until it grew so heavy it fell through the attic and collapsed in his house.

Moral: People who live in grass houses shouldn't stow thrones.

Here is another one which is kind of a puzzle.

Up in Nebraska, some years ago, lived three brothers who were farmers. They raised corn, which they fed to their livestock. One fed corn to cattle, one fed corn to hogs, and one fed his corn to boiler chickens. They were very successful.

One day, they decided to put their three farms together, form a corporation, and operate one big feed business.

They couldn't agree on a name for the venture, so they went to their old mother for advice.

She told them she would call the new business "Focus."

If you think a little about this word "focus," you will discover the old lady's answer was a first class pun.

Roosters

September 1984

For a long time, we have needed roosters around here that would crow vigorously in the early morning. It would supply a cheerful note to the day's beginning. While we sipped our coffee and the bacon sizzled in the skillet, my wife and I could listen to the rooster crow. On pleasant mornings, we could take our coffee on the back porch where we would perhaps see the rooster greet the morning sun from atop a gate post or some such pedestal.

It was with this vision of bucolic tranquility that I readily accepted Betty Pearson's proposition last spring to board a few chickens. Up until that time, I had never heard of anyone boarding chickens, but after Betty, one of Major County's leading poultry persons, explained the situation, it all seemed perfectly logical and a very cheap way to get hold of a high-dollar rooster. Two high-dollar roosters, as it turned out.

The two roosters came with eighteen hens. All of these chickens were 100 percent purebred brown Leghorns, and the reason for isolating them on this farm was so the hens would have no consort with other roosters, and, thereby, in time (after three weeks), produce fertile eggs which could be incubated and hatched into more 100 percent purebred brown Leghorn chickens. Simple.

We set these birds up with regular Hilton Inn, Class A accommodations. New straw on the floor, and in the nests, a large pen with grass and shade, fresh water, and self-feeder full of expensive mash. And sure enough, on the first day in their new home, the hens laid ten eggs.

All summer long, these hens have average thirteen to fourteen eggs every day. Our refrigerator is loaded with eggs. Sometimes, my wife has to throw out leftovers two or three days before she normally would just to make room for more eggs.

The roosters are not acting at all like I thought they would. They are discontented and under stress all the time. They want the hens to lay more eggs. They spend 99 percent of their time persuading the hens to go into the nest boxes and lay more eggs. One percent of their time, they are doing what normal roosters do. The rest of the time they are herding hens.

My wife detests the roosters. She calls them male chauvinists. Sometimes, she uses unladylike expletives. "Look at that danged rooster," she will say, "He is going to worry the life out of that hen. He just hit her! Pecked her right in the rib!"

The trouble with the roosters results from a physical defect. Neither one of them has a tail. This throws off their balance and makes them walk (strut) in an unnatural tilted-back position. It makes them self-conscious. Gives them a complex. They have to try harder. We call them Avis I and Avis II.

The worst thing about the roosters is that they don't crow much. They are so exhausted after a day's work, they sleep late and their crowing is nothing but a pitiful half-hearted squawk. I fear it may be the death of them.

Rubik's Cube

"The Rubik Cube is a remarkable puzzle invented by the Hungarian sculptor, designer, and architectural engineer Erno Rubik of the School for Commercial Artists in Budapest."

That is the opening sentence of a thirty-page booklet which outlines one series of maneuvers for solving the puzzle.

I am sure that Professor Rubik knew he was designing something clever when he designed the puzzle, but surely, he never imagined the millions of hours people would spend fiddling with his invention.

Several books and pamphlets have been written giving hints and instructions for solving the puzzle. Mathematicians write treatises on the thing and amuse each other by devising new approaches to solving the puzzle.

Rubik's Cube has swept the world. There are people, mostly young people, who have become very adept and very fast at solving it.

Last summer, my daughter gave me one of the cubes. I toyed with it twenty minutes and announced no solution was possible. Then I read in the paper that some child could fix the puzzle in ninety seconds. Later, I heard on the radio that some kid in New Jersey could slide the puzzle in correct position in twenty-nine seconds. Just last night, I saw a youth do it in twenty-six seconds.

I will not be surprised when I learn that someone has done it in nothing flat with one hand tied behind his back.

By carefully following the instructions in the booklet again and again and again, I solved Rubik's Cube in six hours and forty five minutes. I won't get any faster because I don't intend to do it again.

My wife calls my accomplishment a tribute to bull-headed stubbornness. I like to think of it as a demonstration of diligence and dexterity.

After all, there are probably quite a few people who couldn't sit down and twiddle their fingers for six hours and forty five minutes.

Sacajawea: Heroine

December 4, 1980

Sacajawea was an Indian lady who accompanied the Lewis and Clark expedition on their famous hike across the continent back in 1803, 1804, and 1805. According to someone's reckoning, there have been more statues erected to her than to any other American woman. She is usually depicted standing on a breezy hilltop with a papoose slung across her back, her arm outstretched pointing the way to the Pacific Ocean. Looking at one of these statues, you are left with your imagination to picture Lewis and Clark and all the other troops toiling up the mountainside trying to keep up with Sacajawea, the guide. A heroic figure, indeed.

I have reached page 874 of a book entitled *Sacajawea*. I am going to lay it aside and wait until spring to finish the remaining 468 pages. It was written by Anna Waldo who claims it took her ten years, and I can certainly believe that.

Sacajawea was a heroic figure, but, of course, she didn't know that. Neither Lewis nor Clark knew that. They didn't know they were heroic people. They and the men who accompanied them were all just doing a little job for Tom Jefferson, the president. Mr. Jefferson wanted to know how big the country was that he presided over. What was out there beyond the Mississippi? Could men travel overland to the Pacific Ocean?

Well, they could, and they did, and Sacajawea is getting a lot of belated credit for the success of the expedition.

In a way, it is a fanciful tale. Mrs. Waldo spins a long, long yarn based on conjecture, and in some places, mighty little historical evidence. Yet, when you read this book, you sometimes read between the lines, and it is easy to believe that it all happened just the way Mrs. Waldo says it did.

It is commonly thought today that we live our lives intensely. We travel fast and far to do things in a hurry. We accomplish things our forebears never dreamed of. We live a lot more than our ancestors did.

Maybe not. Consider this. Lewis and Clark were both in their twenties when the expedition began. Most of the troops (it was considered a military expedition) were in their teens or early twenties. Sacajawea is believed to have been about fifteen years old when they started.

Somewhere in Minnesota, or thereabouts, she gave birth to a male child. It didn't hold them up long. She carried little Jean Baptiste on her back to the Pacific Ocean and back to the village of St. Louis.

The oldest man on the trip was Sacajawea's man, Charbonneau, a half-breed Frenchman. He was in his forties and was apparently a worthless cuss traveling along as an interpreter and throwing in the labors of his squaw to boot, free of charge.

If you know anybody that likes to read this kind of stuff, you can get a paperback copy of the book *Sacajawea* for $3.95. That's what I call a reasonably priced Christmas present.

Shootout Fairview State Bank, 1935

January 1988

In February 1935, Dale Stamphill escaped from Granite Reformatory where he was serving twenty years for armed robbery.

Seeking revenge on Irv Brewer, Fairview's night watchman, he traveled north with two companions: Mallory "Red" Kuykendall serving seventy-five years for armed robbery and W. L. Baker Jr., serving fifteen years for manslaughter.

They arrived very early in the morning and parked their car in the alley in back of what is now Napa Store.

Stamphill and Kuykendall walked up the street and secluded themselves in a stairwell near the Ourway Café where they waited for Brewer to finish his morning coffee.

When Brewer stepped out of the door onto the sidewalk, Stamphill announced himself. "Hey, Irv," he shouted. "I'm back."

Brewer and Stamphill were well acquainted. No further communication was necessary. Irv dived under a Model A pickup parked at the curb, and all of the participants of this confrontation blasted away with their revolvers.

This duel raged for as long as it takes to empty three revolvers, whereupon the assailants fled back to their car and escaped—for the time being. The Model-A had seven or eight holes in its side, and it was later revealed that Kuykendall had a bullet in the butt.

One wild shot pierced the plate glass window of the Fairview State Bank. A neat hole. About three feet from the front door and six feet above the sidewalk. Eye catching to the bank's customers.

Floyd Perkins, president of the bank, was a conservative man. He patched the hole with two big washers and a stove bolt. Total cost of the repair: three cents. The repair job lasted until 1948 when somebody else remodeled the building.

For thirteen years, the patched bullet hole reminded the citizens of two important realities:

1. Unexpected things will happen.
2. The bank does not waste money on nonessentials.

Floyd Perkins knew about subliminal messages long before Madison Avenue had a word for it.

Short Tall Tales

July 11, 1980

Jay Kliewer had a strange experience last week. He and his crew were running casing into a new well out in the blackjacks west of town one hot afternoon. The temperature was about 102 degrees when a small cloud drifted over and surprised them with a sprinkle of rain. One of the floor hands fainted. Jay says he finally had to get a hardhat full of dry sand and toss it in the fellow's face to get him revived.

Is that a tall story? I'm not sure. It seems to me that a hatful of dry hot sand thrown in a fellow's face would be just as shocking as a hatful of cold water.

The summer wears on. Ray Keeton is digging potatoes and hauling dirt to his garden. His potatoes this year are so large and bountiful, he says, that after he has dug them out, he finds it necessary to haul in dirt to fill up the holes.

Charles Knight still hasn't figured out a way to outwit the giant catfish he had been stalking for several seasons. His last plan of attack was just as unsuccessful as earlier ones. This is a big fish he is after. Maybe fifty or forty pounds.

The fish lives in a big hole on the North Canadian River. In the bottom of the hole is an old car body. That is where the fish sleeps. He has been baited with every kind of lure known to fishermen. He has been hooked but never caught. He tears up everything and gets away every time.

The last attempt to catch the fish involved hand fishing. "Noodling" is what it is called on the Illinois River. Charles and his buddy went well prepared. They went to get the fish.

They took a hay hook and a long length of stout nylon rope. One end of the rope was tied to a cottonwood tree on the riverbank. Quietly, they eased into the water and dove down to the old car body where they knew the fish would be resting.

The idea was to slip the hook into his gills and get out of the way. They would have him for sure this time.

It didn't work.

The wily old sucker had rolled up all the windows and locked the doors.

Space Age 1983

The engineering achievements and machines that fill one generation with lifelong amazement and wonder become common place and are taken for granted by the next generation.

Although my father owned twenty five or thirty cars in his lifetime and drove them hundreds of thousands of miles, he never ceased to marvel at the efficiency of the automobile. To him, it was forever a miraculous invention.

"Imagine!" he would say, "I drove my new car all the way to Colorado Springs and never added one drop of oil to the engine. Listen to that motor! Eighty miles an hour and you can barely hear it hum. The crankshaft is perfect. Every bearing is an absolute fit. I don't know how they do it!"

He remembered a childhood of cantankerous horses, bouncing wagons with no springs and wooden wheels that had to be pulled loose and greased every few miles.

It is different with me. The only time an automobile amazes me is when it runs out of gasoline or won't start on a cold morning.

The machines that intrigue me most are man-made satellites. I don't know how they do it. I will never have anything but the vaguest idea of how they get up there or how they are controlled.

October marks the twenty-sixth anniversary of the launching of the first orbiting satellite, Sputnik! It was a silver-clad sphere weighing 184 pounds when the Russians put it into orbit October 4, 1957. It was dumbfounding news. As I remember it, most people thought it was a hoax and didn't believe it until President Eisenhower verified it in an official press release.

Since that day, thousands of satellites of various shapes and sizes have been launched. Altogether, 180 astronauts and cosmonauts have gone aloft. Twelve Americans have actually landed their marvelous machines on the moon and shuffled around in that ancient dust. Almost unbelievable.

Consider the facts. First man to orbit in space, Yuri Gagarin, 1961; first American in space, Alan Shepherd, May, 1961; first people on the moon, Neil Armstrong and Edwin Aldrin, July 20, 1969. The Russians have had two accidents in space. Four men died. The first manned space flight exceeded six months. The Soviets plan to have a permanent twelve-man station in orbit by 1985.

If you don't think that is all pretty amazing, you probably belong to the Pac-Man, Asteroid Defender generation.

The Art of Farming

Dad checking his wheat

In the economic scheme of things, there are technicians, craftsmen, professionals, warriors, and artists. Everyone knows where he fits in the scheme. Doctors, lawyers, and preachers call themselves professionals. Carpenters call themselves craftsmen while electricians and airplane pilots are technicians. Soldiers and grunt laborers are warriors. Musicians and actors are artists.

When you are a farmer, you can get up in the morning and fit the day to suit your fancy. You get to do your own classification. Label the job to suit yourself.

You go out and plow a field. You look at the field and you look at the plow and go into the work with whatever attitude you choose.

One of my neighbors is an artist. I doubt he knows it. Everything he does is with the artists' view. He lays out fence, furrows, fields, and terraces, and they all blend into balance. A beautiful farm. He does it all so easily, like a spider spinning a web.

Another neighbor goes into a field like an infantryman into battle. In storm and flurry, his crew approaches the field at sundown with tractors, plows, pickups, CB radios, shouts of instructions, and a general hullabaloo. Whamming and driving all night long. By morning, the field is conquered and all the paraphernalia is gone.

Another friend of mine might fiddle around two weeks getting ready a forty-acre field to plant cotton. He won't get up too early. Won't work very late. Spends lots of time adjusting the equipment. Sensibly rests after the noon meal. And so on. He is a technician.

I know another kind of farmer. He lives in Enid and farms in Amarillo. Inherited land. His biggest expenses are telephone calls and memo pads. He is in daily (hourly) contact with the "operators." He classifies himself a professional.

Then there are the craftsman farmers. It is something they do on the side. Another job. They are mostly ex-farm boys taking care of the family fields, usually because Dad or Grandpa thinks they ought to.

They really don't care too much about farming, but the money's not too bad for the time it takes, so they do it. And they do a good job of it because it's another craft they learned long ago in their childhood.

Telephone, Tips, and Cigarettes

Whenever the government passes a big tax bill, it always gouges some people more than others. The ninety-eight-billion-dollar bill that Mr. Reagan and Mr. O'Neil arranged a couple of weeks ago was no exception. The President called it a "revenue enhancement bill." I thought that was a nice way to put it. Kind of like saying someone "passed on" when what you mean is, "He died."

The bill doubles the Federal tax on cigarettes to sixteen cents per pack; it triples the tax on telephones, and it sics the IRS onto waiters and waitresses who receive cash tips.

If you happen to be a cigarette-smoking waitress with a telephone, you may be in for dark days and hard times.

There are a few waiters working in fancy restaurants around the country who make a nice living pocketing tips from high rollers. Maybe they don't pay income tax on their tips. I don't know.

Most of the people waiting on tables are teenage girls or middle-aged ladies working for less than minimum wages. Now, Congress is whipping up the IRS to go chasing after a cut on the dimes and quarters left on the table by satisfied customers.

That's kind of like sending a Sherman tank out to get a rabbit.

I don't want to do without a telephone, so I will pay the added Federal tax when it comes to my bill. Maybe the government will funnel some of the tax money back to Ma Bell so she can hire more crews to search out frequent short circuits.

How are they going to raise the money? I can tell you. They are going to collect it from us, cigarette smokers. Yes, sir, it is the health-damaged, weak-lunged, weed-burning addicts that are going to cough up most of that ninety-eight billion dollars, while the healthy taxpayers of the country are out there jogging around in the fresh air and spending idle time nailing up No Smoking signs, the cigarette smoking patriots of the country will be puffing and hacking away on that ninety-eight billion dollar bill.

I guess we could switch to pipes. No tax on pipes. But what kind of courage is that? We can't quit. Our country needs us.

Personally, I feel kind of indebted to the government anyway on this cigarette business. Some decades ago when I worked for the government, part of the deal was free board and room and cheap cigarettes. Ninety cents per carton, nine cents a pack. Reasonable deal.

On days when we worked in the field, they sent us out with box lunches which they called K rations. In each box was a little package of four cigarettes. That was a thoughtful touch, and I always appreciated it.

I am happy to have this chance now to repay the government and help it through this revenue enhancement project.

White Rock

November 6, 1980

Around 1932, two fellows from the Meno area came to Fairview and built a monument to good taste and good times. Art Nolting and Ernie Kuhnemund erected the White Rock Café.

It was equipped with a counter and twelve stools. Back of the counter was the grill, the coffee pot, the chili pot, the bean pot, and cupboards for the crockery. Under the counter were the soda pop, the cracker box, and the cash drawer. Nolting left the business in a year or so, and Ernie ran the joint until after World War II.

Even today when I get a whiff of frying onions, an image of the old White Rock Café flashes through my mind, and my salivary glands begin to overwork. In the White Rock Café, you took your hamburgers with fried onions or raw onions and you lathered on the mustard with a wooden paddle. Lettuce, mayonnaise, tomatoes, and such other decorations hadn't been invented yet.

The chili was so savory it defies description. During World War II, when lads from this community met anywhere in the world, it wasn't long before they discussed the true value of a bowl of White Rock chili. Traveling salesmen, I am told, used to schedule overnight stops in Fairview just so they could sup and breakfast on White Rock chili.

Over the years, the place changed a little from time to time. When 3.2 beer was legalized, some remodeling was necessary. About 1940, a storeroom was added on the back, and, eventually, two or three booths were installed.

Some people called it a beer joint. Some called it a hamburger joint, and some called it a chili joint. Mostly though, it was just called White Rock.

Ernie opened it up at 5 a.m. and closed it at 11 p.m. seven days a week. Hamburgers cost five cents, with onions or without onions, fried or raw. Chili cost ten cents, with or without beans. A bowl of oyster crackers and a glass of water was part of the deal. In the 1930s, you could get a decent lunch for fourteen cents. For five cents more, you got a Nehi orange or an RC Cola (RC Cola packed about three ounces more in a bottle than Coca-Cola did). If a fellow was feeling real flush, he could fork up another nickel and top off the lunch with a Mr. Goodbar that weighed about a quarter of a pound.

On special days, like Old Settlers Day or Trades Day, hamburgers were six for a quarter. On one memorable day, Mush McCue tells me, Ernie slapped 144 dozen hamburgers.

Cash was awfully short during the Depression and lunch at the White Rock was a real treat. I knew a couple of lucky kids that got seventy-five cents allowance and ate lunch there every school day of the week.

We had one rich kid in town, Doc McCroski's only child, Bobby. Bobby always had a pocketful of nickels and dimes.

He passed through childhood, adolescence, and adulthood eating nothing but White Rock chili and Mr. Goodbars (plus an occasional peck or so of gumdrops and chocolates). He was addicted to the joint. He could not pass it by. It drew him in. And little wonder. On a still day, you could smell those frying onions and that simmering chili two blocks away.

I just realized that we cannot talk about the White Rock in a newspaper column. What we need is some kind of White Rock Café Convention where we could gather up enough material to write some books.

Three Farms

The Internal Revenue Service and I have been working together like a well-broken team. With the help of Dean Wymer, we have got all the forms filled out that their best IRS people could find to send us. The IRS has temporarily run out of forms (they will send more just as soon as they get them printed). In the meantime, I am spending my time in a worthwhile manner. I am counting greenbugs in the wheat and catching up on my reading.

I just finished *Three Farms* by Mark Kramer. It is one of the best books I have ever read.

It is the story of three modern American farms. The subtitle of the book is *Making Milk, Meat, and Money from the American Soil*. It is a short book of 274 pages.

In addition to being a clear and easy reading writer, the author has done his homework. From a farmer's point of view, the writer is unusually correct with his details. He doesn't overwhelm us with statistics. On the other hand, he doesn't get his bushels, acres, and dollars mixed up either.

Mr. Kramer writes about a Massachusetts dairy farm, an Iowa corn and hog farm, and a large corporate tomato farm in California. He tells exactly how they operate. He discusses the people, the labor, the machinery, the money, and, yes, the manure.

He knows his history. Much of the fascination of this book comes from the comparison of how it was in the past and how it is now.

There is, of course, a lot of political and social significance to the rapidly changing conditions in American agriculture. The technological changes that have so greatly increased our production, and, at the same time, reduced the number of people actually farming, can be seen all around us.

No one yet knows what effect the rapidly developing corporate management of truck farming in California will have on the cost and supply of our food. The author refers to this as "farmer-less farming."

In the book *Three Farms*, Mr. Kramer does not suggest solutions or recommend changes. He does not simplify complex situations. Like Jack Webb, the old TV detective, he just lays out the facts—and entertains us to boot.

Interesting Things Heard at Trade's Day

Loafing around Trade's Day grounds last Monday, I finally asked my old friend why he keeps buying those old broken down stoves and refrigerators.

So, he told me.

"In the first place," he said, "they are cheap. A good many of these items, most of these items, could be very useful and functional with very little repair and clean-up. We live in a wasteful society. A lot of the goods thrown away today are better than what replaces them."

"Then there is metal," he continued, "the real value."

I knew I was set up for another lesson in economics and political philosophy.

"That stove has several pounds of cast iron on it. It has some brass and copper in it, and over one hundred pounds of steel. Base metals. All of it is just as good as it ever was. Heat the metal and it can be reshaped or cast into a million other forms. All it takes is work and heat. The Japanese showed us that back in the 1940s. They came here in the 1930s and hauled away thousands of ship loads of our junk. We called it junk. They knew better."

"Yep. They hauled it away and heated it. They shaped it into airplanes, machine guns, tanks, and rifles….they made a war machine. And they very nearly whipped us with our old stoves and broken down cars. They would have whipped us if they had just made a bigger plan before they started."

"Base metal. The true value. Nations rise and fall depending on how they handle base metals."

The lesson went on.

"We have a lot of money in this country. People value it. What is it? Paper with numbers and a picture printed on it. Politicians declare its value in the first place and in the end, politicians prove its worthlessness."

"Gold has its place. You can fill a hollow tooth with it, or shape it into a shiny bauble. The best use for it though is trade. You can trade it for base metals. Then you can make machines… automobiles, tractors, plows, and if need be, tools of war. Shucks. You can even make stoves and refrigerators with it."

With that, he laughed and bid another on another old stove for a dollar and a quarter.

The Universal Slip

I have a wife, three grown daughters, and one daughter-in-law. You would think I have heard about every conceivable problem a lady can have with her clothes. Not so. On Sunday morning, I overheard a discussion on the subject of slitted underslips.

At first, I thought the girls were playing some sort of word game. While reading the newspaper in the next room, I kept hearing the words "single-slitted slip" and "double-slitted slip" drift out of the conversation at the breakfast table.

What they were talking about, it turns out, was the proper kind of underslip to be worn with a slitted skirt or dress.

For those of you who do not know about slitted skirts, let me tell you what little I know. The slitted skirt idea is a fashion gimmick that is rediscovered from time to time as the years roll by. It first appeared in China several centuries ago where, for all I know, it is still high fashion today. The classic design of this fashion is a skinny, ankle-length dress with the skirt slit up the side to about the knee.

The original purpose of the slits was to unhobble the wearer of this tight narrow dress and thus enable her to walk.

That is not the problem with the ladies, I know. The problem I hear about is underslips to fit the slits in the skirts—or the absence of slits in the skirts.

"All you really need," said one daughter "is a two-slit slip. You can wear them with any kind of skirt."

"No," said another daughter. "If you wear a two-slit slip with a dress of sheer material, it will look as if you have some sort of loin cloth flapping around under your dress."

And what if you wear a skirt that is slit only in the front or back? The slits are in the wrong place.

What we need is three-slit slip. How about a four-slit slip? Might as well wear a grass skirt then.

"Why wear the dumb things at all?" said the youngest daughter.

"What do you mean? The skirts or the slips?"

"The slips. Why wear the slips?"

"Because your mother told you to always wear an underslip. That's why."

With that remark, the conversation moved to another topic.

The problem challenged me. What the world needs as a universal underslip. I believe I've got it worked out.

Just as soon as I can get some financial backing, I am going to start manufacturing four-slit underslips. Each slit will be equipped with a zipper.

The slip can be then arranged simply by opening or closing zippers to fit with any type of skirt a lady might choose to wear.

It is such a simple idea. I am surprised no one has thought of it before now.

On the other hand, there still remains the problem of length. A truly universal underslip would have to be adjustable for length. Different length skirts require different length underslips.

I will have to give this thing more thought.

White-Knuckle Flying

There are people who will not get into an airplane. Under no circumstances will they allow themselves to be closed into such a flimsy and illogical piece of machinery. Common sense tells them that if apples fall out of trees, airplanes will fall out of the sky. They usually do not care to discuss the subject at all. As far as they are concerned, any successful takeoff and landing of an aircraft is just another accident.

These people do not take chances with the whims of God or tricks of the devil. They simply don't get into airplanes.

Then there are people known as "white-knuckle flyers" that will pay good money for an airline ticket, climb aboard, and fly for hours scared to death every inch of the way. These are people who believe they have thrown common sense out of the window and that they live by faith alone. They, too, know all about Sir Isaac Newton and the apples. They also believe that every successful takeoff and landing is a kind of accident. But they have faith. They believe God will permit at least one more accident to occur. They pray before flying and after flying.

I enjoy flying and am perfectly at ease most of the time. I don't mind, however, spotting a white-knuckle flyer when I get on a plane. It can't hurt anything. Having someone aboard who is spending all his time communicating with a higher power certainly can't hurt anything.

My wife is a white-knuckle flyer. The minute the airport comes into view, anxiety breaks out on her like sunburn on a blonde. That's not quite true. It doesn't show much anymore. She loves to travel and over the years, she has learned to control most of the visible signs of fear—paleness, trembling hands, quavering voice. All those things are gone. She has even passed beyond the need for sedatives. No more tranquilizers, no pills, no booze.

Her anxiety now comes out in more subtle ways.

I overheard her asking a ticket agent recently if their airline furnished information showing the relative experience of the pilots—age, years of training, number of accidents, and so forth.

She once got off a plane that was ready to go because the overhead baggage compartment wouldn't fasten shut. When someone from the flight crew came up and taped it shut with duct tape, my wife got off. "If that's the way they fix a broken latch," she said, "I can just imagine how they keep the wings on—baling wire, most likely."

On our last trip, we were seated, all buckled down, ready for takeoff. My wife was in her usual position for takeoff—hands gripping tightly on the ends of the arm rests, one knee firmly braced on the seat in front, the other leg stiff with her foot wedged against the wall, eyes closed, head bowed.

Everything seemed in perfect readiness.

Then I noticed she was trying to say something. I bent my head to her and she whispered, "Have you noticed that this airplane has three rows of seats on the right side but only two rows of seats on the left side? Won't that unbalance it? Won't that cause it to roll over to the right when we take off?"

I explained to her that when they arrange the seats that way, they always make the right wing ten feet longer than the left wing and that balances everything out in good shape.

She nodded understandingly. "Thank you," she whispered. "They ought to explain things like that to children in grade school."

Observations and Musings

Introduction to McWilliam Davis, Storyteller

by Assunta Martin

McWilliam Davis was a storyteller and a recorder of the history of his times throughout his life. His stories about routine activities in a small community in Oklahoma were thoughtful, entertaining, and insightful. Known by many in his community as the Will Rogers of Major County, McWilliam Davis entertained many with his humor column, "Notes from a Farmer."

He was also a prolific letter writer, and to receive a letter from Mac was a much-awaited treat. His family treasures the reams of musings, letters, observations, and running commentaries that Mac, as he was known by all, churned out in his loopy, elegant penmanship on his favored legal-size yellow pads.

The letters he wrote often express a side of Mac that was not often evident in the humor columns published for the community he loved and knew so well. Much of Mac's writing was done in the winter, a time in Oklahoma when farmers tend to maintenance, fencing, and other chores while they wait patiently for the thick green young winter wheat to carpet the hard-worked and well-tilled earth.

In 1997, Mac died at the young age of seventy-four. His loss is still felt by his family and by his community. Many of his columns have been recycled and printed again in recent years.

Going through the many stacks and boxes of writings, I recently came across this passage written on one of his familiar yellow pads.

From time to time, I think about my life as it has occurred and I am intrigued and sometimes puzzled about it. I think of stories my mother and father have told me. I remember vaguely family stories my Grandmother Davis related. I remember vividly the stories my grandmother McCue repeated. Grandma McCue lived to be an ancient lady, and in her last years, she retold and retold. My old father does the same thing now, and I suppose if I live to an old age I will do the same thing.

What I set out here to do is to put down some of the events and situations of my life as I recall them in meditative intervals, with the idea that it might be of some interest later on to some child or grandchild. And, who knows, it might even be of some interest to myself later on!

The usual way to go at a thing like this is chronologically. However since my thoughts of the past do not come like that, I won't be doing it that way. So a tale of the 1930s might follow a tale of the 1980s. Right now, I am thinking about land and money and the day I went off to the big war. Old double-u, eye, eye, as Lawrence Welk once called it while reading off cue cards on his TV show.

On January 13, 1943, they swore me in, and on January 20, my twentieth birthday, I reported for duty down at Fort Sill, Oklahoma, the most sophisticated and largest artillery school in the entire world at that time. Anyway, that's what they told us then. I suspect now that both the Germans and the Russians had some artillery schools just about equal to Fort Sill.

When I left Fairview early that morning, I got on a bus with about twenty-five to thirty other young bucks. We loaded up in front of the Floyd Hotel (where Tincey's is now). There was quite a crowd there. Most everybody's parents were there and a lot of townspeople too.

My uncle Jacob Davis was there and that surprised me, and when he shook my hand, tears were running down his face and that puzzled me. Uncle Jacob was a veteran of World War I, and later on, of course, I understood the tears.

My father always said Uncle Jacob was very sentimental. And so he might have been. For certain, he knew things on that day that most of the people there didn't know.

On the day before I left, I gave my father $4,200. It was genuine cash money deposited in the Farmer's and Merchant's Bank. I told him to take the money and buy some land. I'm not sure about that statement. More likely, he said, "I'll take the money and buy you some land." I have never, until recently, thought I had any significant money. I have always had money. I have always lived, not poor, but extremely modestly. I have never in my life been broke, but I have been down to a very few bucks.

A digression—a small digression to the story. One time in 1949, after the war, when I was going to school at Oklahoma University, I thought I was dead broke. No money for grub. I had a wife and small kid. Problem. I went down to the Norman pawnshop and handed them a rifle out from my clothes closet. The man gave me twenty dollars, and I went and stocked up on groceries. We feasted on spaghetti with meat sauce. The mail carrier came by that afternoon and be-damned if there wasn't a government check in there for seventy-four dollars back pay the army forgot to give me! Two years out of service and they send me a paycheck for seventy-four dollars! I went back and got the rifle. Fastest two dollars he ever made, the pawnbroker told me.

Back to the story. The old man bought the E 2SW 4 of 22-21-12. It's the eighty acres where the Pizza Hut and all the nice homes now stand. It was farmland then and the price was $7500. High price for those times, but it was good land.

When I went into the army, the pay was fifty dollars per month. It had recently been raised from twenty dollars to fifty. They had some deal going where they could withhold some of this fabulous pay and put it in your bank. I signed up for twenty-eight dollars to be withheld. When I got home four years, eight months, and twenty-two days later, my land was paid off and I had 1,400 odd bushels of wheat in the elevator. I was twenty-five years old.

It is now almost thirty-three years since I finished active military services. No single day has passed that I have not had occasion to recall some part of it. It is always an intellectual, mental recollection. I was never wounded, never scratched, so it is not a physical reminder that comes to me every day, as it does to hundreds of thousands of other people.

The recollections of that time have influenced almost every action of my life. The recollections are sometimes saddening and sometimes joyful, sometimes detrimental and sometimes beneficial. Looking on my life today, I cannot tell the good influence from the bad. I am fair constant. The world is all madness. Some days, the world is all joy. Every day is different. Some days I drink vast amounts of booze. Some months go by with no booze. In those months, I drink vast amounts of coffee and water.

This writing is not meant to be an analysis of self. It is meant to be a chronicle of stories.

My mother's name was McCue. Hazel Irene McCue. She was, physically, a very gentle woman. I cannot remember a single time she ever touched me with a violent hand or even raised her voice to me. She was quick of wit and might say something that was incomprehensible for two days. Then it would come to me, I had been chastised.

She finished high school in Fairview, Oklahoma, around the year 1918. She became a schoolteacher, qualified by one summer term at the college in Alva. She went to school that summer with Emma Wenger, who later became my Aunt Emma, when she married Uncle Jacob, my father's older brother.

She taught at Progressive School. She ran the Progressive School when she was eighteen years old. She had about forty students. They ranged in age from five to nineteen. The nineteen-year-olds were male and it was no easy job.

Progressive schoolhouse was five miles from the town where her parents lived. Too far away to live at home. She boarded, first with the Grunan's, where she slept on a corn-shuck mattress. Then she boarded with my grandma Davis where she slept in a carpeted upstairs room on a bed with a goose-down tick.

My grandma Davis was widowed at the age of thirty-two, when her husband, William, died of a fever. It must have been scarlet fever. In the last weeks of his suffering, his mind deranged, they hauled him away to an asylum in Norman, Oklahoma. My grandma Davis was left with the farm and the sons aged six, eight, and ten.

She never remarried and as far as I've heard, never entertained any suitors. She was noted around the county as a good cook, a pillar in the Methodist church, and a sound manager of her farm.

She died in her fifties and left 320 acres of land to her sons and a $5,000 mortgage on it. She died in the early 1930s, but it took my father and uncles a long time to pay off the mortgage.

If they quarreled or fussed about how to divide the land, I never heard about it. For certain, no lawyers or judges had much to do with it. I think they met one Sunday afternoon and decided who was entitled to what. The abstracts of the title to the land reveal simple settlements amongst them.

This is part of an, alas, unfinished piece. Thankfully though, there are many such commentaries, and when read together, a narrative emerges. It is a narrative written on nicely lined yellow paper, as well as backs of envelopes and brown paper bags. When not writing or farming, Mac read voraciously. When the old farmhouse was remodeled and expanded, a room designated as the "library room" housed hundreds of books, novels, numerous periodicals, and countless rolls of maps and charts.

This is not to say that his life was a smooth sail over a serene lake. Mac was an alcoholic for many years, and many of his writings reflect his thoughts and conflicted feelings about that.

At the age of fifty-seven, in 1980, Mac and his wife both went into a treatment center and successfully conquered their demons. As recovering alcoholics, both dedicated untold hours to the sponsoring and mentoring of other alcoholics. Their doors were always open, and no desperate call went unanswered.

Mac was an observer of life. He suffered no more nor less than others, but through the twisted spins and curves that living a full life necessarily brings, he always exuded a warmth and deep personal interest in the people around him. His talent at accepting the imperfections of himself and of others allowed him to find humor in situations that many would simply find frustrating and distressing. Eager to listen, Mac could work a story out of even the most reticent and tongue-tied in the community.

Some of the following stories, musings, letters and observations were intended to be developed into longer stories, and some are stand-alone anecdotes or comments.

The Great Depression

One sad story from the 1930s.

The grimness of some childhood experiences does not impact upon our wonderment of life until middle age. A few years ago, I was visiting with a childhood friend of the depression era. She told me a story of childhood, kind of offhand but very serious also. A story she had not often told, maybe never told because it was just the way things happened. The reality of life—never thought of as a story until late in life.

Here it is.

She was one of the younger children in a large, close knit, independent, hard-working family living on a hard scrabble farm where the Gloss Mountains break down into gulches and gullies before the fertile flatlands where we grow the wheat. Subsistence farming, with a cotton-tail or jack rabbit thrown into the stew pot pretty often. This is what she told me:

"My mother died in childbirth. It was her tenth child. I was next to the youngest. Baby was only two and I was six. The older boys were almost grown. It was hard. We just kind of raised each other. My brothers were so good to us young ones, but it was hard. My mother died. The baby was alive. It was so weak and so tiny and there was no milk, no one to feed it. My father said, he said, let it go too. We can not take care of it."

"A hard time." I said.

" Yes," she said, "but the rest of us made it okay."

A Mutilated Ear

On Monday, in a freak accident too bizarre to explain, I stabbed myself with a plow shear and mutilated my left ear. It was immediately obvious that a little disinfectant and a Band-Aid were not going to fix it, so my brother-in-law hauled me in to Dr. Boughan.

My brother-in-law's idea of first aid was to hand me a wad of bloody Kleenex as we walked into Dr. Boughan's office.

"Here," he said, "scatter these around as we walk in. That will get their attention and we won't have to wait. Try to bleed on the receptionist's desk, that will hurry her along. Those people hate blood in the waiting room."

Dr. Boughan's bedside manner is especially up and jocular when he is examining what the medical folks term minor cuts, burns, bruises, and abrasions.

"If you are planning to wear an earring in this ear," he said, "you have overdone the piercing."

"Humph."

"Ears are easy," he said, getting into his surgical rig (green smock and cap). "They heal up fast as a clavicle."

"Wonderful," said I, trying to remember where and what the clavicle is.

"I once sewed an ear back on a young girl from out by Seiling. It was hanging by a shred, and two years later, you couldn't see a stitch mark! Now, this will sting a little bit, but you can handle it. Got some bleeders here we gotta tie off. There is a regular surgeon in the hospital today, over from Enid. I thought about calling him to do this, but I need the money more than he does."

Note: *The re-attached ear healed up just fine, and he could wiggle it just like the other one.*

Apathy

There seems to be an apathy upon everything. I wonder if it just me, or is it really everything and everybody. Nobody seems to be hopping, fighting, mad about anything, and nobody seems to be even mildly enthused, curious, excited, or carried away with anything. Dull.

Politics stimulates about as much interest as yesterday's pancakes. Sports are blah. Learning is back to the same spiz as running through the multiplication tables. Hard to find a book to read. Magazines are mostly zip, flip, zap things.

I look around and everybody seems to be in the same mood. I wonder if the country has been gassed with some slugify breeze.

Maybe it is the weather. No, that's been so miserable that normally people would at least be in a bad mood—snarly like. Not so.

I think somebody pulled the fizz plug and everybody and everything has gone flat, like day-old coke.

Auctions and Auctioneers

November 8, 1969

Attached to an auction sale receipt.

I thought this interesting, but of course all auctions are interesting. There is a kind of real-life drama about them with a lot of applied psychology flying around. And at a really good auction of any kind, if it is properly conducted, there is always quite a lot of humor—sometimes subtle, but usually more on the broad or coarse side. I have observed that good auctioneers are really a kind of actor-producer type characters who try to condition everyone present and do a short scene with them. The good ones are strong on humor. Of course, economics is the name of the game at auctions (and especially cattle auctions). But the humor of life is the thing that makes them go.

Laughter is, after all, about the only single thing that everybody enjoys forever. I just realized again that I missed my slot. I should have been an auctioneer. Meditating again upon the little article, I conclude that Tom K and his brother Hank are not the poles apart they think they are. Hank gets more kicks at a cattle sale than anyone (except a good auctioneer) and yet the surface reason for him being there is all economic—buying, selling, working the sale. Serious type. But he grins and chortles more than most, and gets lots of kicks.

Kicking all that gold back and forth without any paper works is satisfying. It's simpler if everybody just does what he says he will do—of course you have to discipline yourself as to what you will say.

I do not know how it goes at all at most auctions. But I do know about cattle auctions and land auctions. You cannot tell by appearances who has got the money nor who will do the bidding and the buying.

At cattle auctions, you will see a lot of chaps in $40 hats and $50 boots. They will be spiffy clean in blue jeans and plain color (sophisticated) shirts. Plaids and the razzmatazz buttons are out now with the cowboys.

The guy buying the cattle, however, will be some ancient know-it-all in rundown plowshoes, wearing a faded-blue pair of overalls—the bib of which is bulging with sale tickets.

At land sales, there will always be some banker types standing around with black suits and up-to-mod ties, but the guy that makes the final bid will be a tired looking guy wearing about two dollars worth of clothes.

Bottle Calves

When a dairy cow calves, the calf is taken away from her after a day or so and thus becomes an orphan. If it happens to be a female and of good breeding, the dairyman pens it in a nursery and bottle-feed it until it can graze and feed itself. He keeps it for a replacement for his milking herd.

If the orphan happens to be a bull, it is usually sold to some ambitious wheat farmer down the road who believes that raising a few bottle calves is an excellent spare time activity for his wife and children. Such an activity, he thinks, will teach the children responsibility and compassion. Washing and sterilizing the bottles also, he thinks, will help to fill in the spare time his wife has to kill in between fixing the meals, doing the laundry, and so forth.

The wheat farmer encourages his family with this proposition by showing his family with paper and pencil just how profitable the endeavor will be for everyone involved in it.

His part in this scheme, he thinks, is to make arrangements for the calves, the bottles, the dry milk, and quarters for the calves. He is also in charge of instructions on the milk mixing and the cleaning, etc.

After the routine is established, the farmer-entrepreneur plans to go about his other business until the calves are ready to graze for their nourishment. At this point, he will kick them out on wheat pasture or good grass for a few months, and then he'll gather them in and sell them for a tidy sum, which, of course, everybody in the family will naturally benefit from.

It is one of the slickest ideas a wheat farmer could come up with, and every one of them, I know, has not only come up with this idea—he has tried it two or three times. A good idea is worth nothing until you take action on it. Everybody knows that.

Here is a list of things that can happen with the plan to let the kids bottle-feed a few calves:

Two days after you get the calves, the school bus reverses its route, and your kids get picked up first this semester. Too early for them to have time to feed the calves. The farmer feeds the calves.

The calves get sick and need two shots a day of the latest miracle juice the vet or druggist is stocking.

The wife announces that her kitchen is no place for calf bottles and nipples. The farmer builds a wash basin in the barn.

Basketball season arrives, and daylight saving time goes into effect. The children come home at dark. Too late to feed the calves.

Twenty percent of the calves lie down and die for no apparent reason.

One calf is a dwarf.

Buffalo Story

Historians tell us that the Cheyennes were among the greatest horsemen the world has known. Up until the 1880s, they roamed the plains from Dakota to Texas hunting buffalo. The buffalo furnished them the basics of life—food, clothing, shelter, weapons, and fuel. For centuries, the buffalo was fundamental to the Cheyenne culture.

Even today, we can suppose that, to a man of Cheyenne blood, the sight of a buffalo may stir faint longings for glories of the hunt enjoyed by his ancestors. So here is a buffalo and Indian story.

On the south banks of Canton Lake, there is a pasture fenced in with nine or ten strands of barbed wire nailed to tall, heavy posts. In the pasture is a small herd of buffalo put there by Cheyenne Tribal Authorities for the edification of tourists and the remembrance of things past.

Surrounding Canton Lake are picnic areas and camp sites established by a benevolent government for public use. On hot summer days many people come to the area for one reason and another. But in winter time, few come for any reason at all. Even on bright winter days, the area may be almost isolated.

That describes the scene for the last buffalo hunt in Oklahoma that I know anything about.

Young men the world over, with time on their hands, frequently gather in small groups to idle away long afternoons in friendly company. It sometimes happens that strong beverages and funny cigarettes are freely passed around to aid relaxation and stimulate the conversation. Under such circumstances, sooner or later, hunger arises and all thoughts turn to food.

Two weeks ago, just such a group found itself on the southern shores of Canton Lake, gazing at the buffalo. Amongst the group were descendants of those mightiest of hunters, the Cheyenne buffalo runners.

Who knows how wonderful and creative ideas are born? Who knows from whence comes the nerve and courage to act on a good idea? We can only report the facts. Your own imagination will have to ponder the thinking and fill in the details.

After they shot the buffalo, they found the pasture gate locked and they couldn't get in with their pickup to haul out the meat. But where there is a will there is a way. They shot the lock.

When they got to the buffalo, they discovered that even five men can not lift a dead buffalo. They did not give up, but by then they were in a hurry. They lashed the buffalo's heels together and tied onto the hitch ball of the pickup.

Out on the road, things fell apart.

Clay Chicken

February 9, 1967

Kay is still trying to get through all her cookbooks at least one time. She is a pretty good cook, you know? But she still leaves the old tried and true recipes about three times a week to try something absolutely new.

Frequently, these are very good, occasionally they are fair. They are never bad. I think she throws the really bad ones away. The other day, you would have laughed yourself sick.

She found a recipe for something called baker's clay. This "clay" is made with salt, flour, and water. It is a kind of heavy duty non-edible dough. This is the way she used it: A hen was prepared for roasting and covered up top, bottom, and all around with a great slab of clay. The idea is that this sealed up bird will stew in its own juices and steam.

After the prescribed hours, this thing is hauled out of the oven and set on the table. It looked like a giant loaf of pumpernickel bread, slightly burnt. We sat up to table and Kay produced a mallet with which to crack the clay off the succulent bird. She tapped a few times and nothing happened. She swore a little bit, stood up and really whacked it. Nothing happened. She beat it energetically, nothing happened. Of course, all this time, there were gravel-like flakes and slivers being knocked off, and, in fact, everything on the table was pretty well showered with this debris.

I finally suggested, in my quietest manner, that we take this boulder out onto the porch where we could work on it with some heavy tools—like maybe an ax or a really big hammer. Which we did. Believe it or not, I used a carpenter's hammer and a cold chisel to finally uncase the bird. And once we had the armor plating chiseled away enough to get the hen out, it was indeed the most succulent roast hen I have ever eaten!

A Few Memories: Cowboy Boots

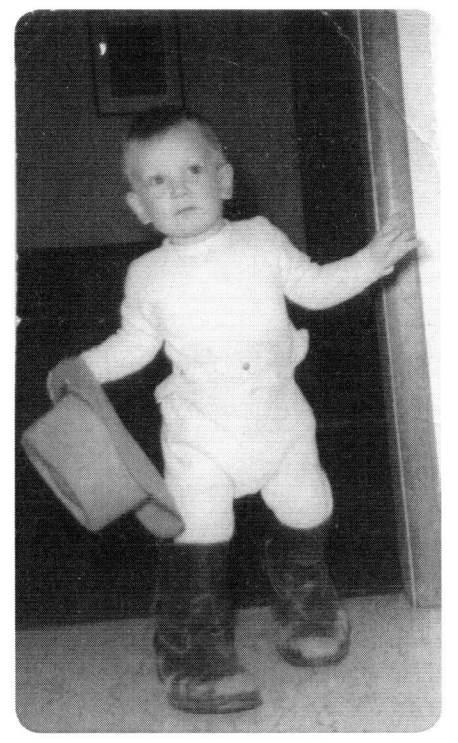

Jess in boots

1978

I want to write this down not because it is any kind of special story but just for the reason that it might be of some interest later on to you and the other 'kinder.'

One short insignificant life put down so to speak on the paper. One little "pluck-out" of the three or five hundred million people that have dried their socks in the same old sunshine as I have.

Mac and Lonnie Morrison moving horses

My young life and my early life—and maybe my whole life—was always influenced by the cowboy image. The cowboy image as written down by Zane Grey and writers of that ilk. Also, when I was very young, like twelve or thirteen, there were still a couple or three real ones hobbling around the town. There were also a lot of phonies, like always, strutting around.

Children pretty early on learn to identify phonies, and I wasn't slow witted, which is to say, I have bought only one pair of pointy-toed boots in my whole life. One pair, you understand. I wouldn't be caught today wearing those killers. I wear flat-heeled and square toe boots in a community where lots of money goes now into lizard skin and otherwise fancy type boots. I still have the old boots stuck back in some corner of the attic. My God, were they fancy. Cost me eighteen bucks in a day when a strong man would dig holes all day long for a buck and a half—and figure he had latched a good deal.

Well, so much for that.

When I was eleven years old, my father, doing the right thing for his child, hired me out to his brother Dawson who made his bread and goods as a wheat farmer.

When I think back upon it, Dawson was an absolutely fantastic human. He taught me everything that he knew and he never raised his voice to me but once (I made some dumb turn with the tractor). In looking back, I think he treated me better than he did his children. And he was pretty good to them too.

The money thing was so important then. The "be careful" and the "waste not" hung like a blanket on all activities. It draped our creativity. It still haunts and warps us all. All of us of that age.

I see myself, I remember myself riding out across the horizon, moving the cattle out to their pasture.

I tell you it was something extraordinary. The horse and I looked like 1870. It was 1935. The hat was black (rejection to phoniness I suppose. No white hat stuff for me, the real thing). The hat was adorned with a band of my own construction. It was a leather thing with bright metal adornments—maybe there was even a small feather, but I'm not sure about that.

Later on, I made a pistol. I whacked it out from a single-shot 22 Caliber rifle. I carried it in my tool box of my tractor when I was eighteen years old and farmed the Poetker 80. It fell out into the field.

I am fifty-three years old, and every time I work that field, I look for that damn pistol. Now that is single-mindedness carried to the extreme.

When I was about thirteen or fourteen, we lived in the town. My father worked at a variety of things. I think he was managing the Knox Auto store when I took over the shoeshine stand at Pool's Barbershop.

It was a pretty good deal. Saturday was the big day. Everybody was in town for Saturday. Haircuts cost thirty-five cents, a shave cost twenty cents, and for a nickel, you could get your shoes shined. On a good day, I would make two dollars. That's forty pairs—a tip was a mighty rare thing. In fact, a lot of customers groused around to be sure they got their money's worth. One coat of liquid polish, two coats of wax, and beaucoup elbow grease. For the privilege of holding this real good position, I had to keep swept up and dusted off. When Curly May came to work there as a barber, I also became a spittoon custodian. Curly chewed tobacco. He usually had a coffee can on the back of the stove. When it got near to full, Orval, the proprietor, would nod to me and I would pitch the can out into the alley and rustle up another can. For some reason that I never understood, they preferred I found Folger coffee cans. Added a little color to the place I suppose. The shoeshine stand was an ancient thing constructed of heavy lumber with the cast iron foot places bolted on to it. It was strong and sturdy and four inches too low. After a long day, which began at 8:00 a.m. and ran till 11:00 a.m., I usually had a backache. But all in all, I thought it was all worthwhile. I always had money in me pocket. In fact, I had a savings account at the Farmers & Merchants Bank.

Bus System in DC

Mac with his '57 Chevy

1960

At the intersection of Georgia and Alaska Avenue, the DC Transit system reaches the limits of its franchise and disgorges there every day several thousand suburbanites leaving them to more or less shift for themselves. Alaska Avenue ends here, but Georgia Avenue runs on out through Silver Spring, Wheaton, Olney, and ends somewhere this side of Philadelphia. It is a main thoroughfare for several hundred thousand people. There are several systems in operation for getting the commuter on down the road. The most reliable one is to be met by someone driving a car. It is not entirely reliable—wives, children, cows, and traffic being sometimes incompatible—but it is the most reliable. There are generally two or three flop-fendered taxicabs willing to transport the commuter out to Wheaton for three or four dollars. They are not always there, but they are generally there. The cabs are of a fairly recent make, some of them being not more than four or five years old. The drivers, however, are much older. The average age must be fifty-five or so. They have survived by taking it easy. There are two other ways left for the traveler. He can hitchhike. The hitching is sometimes not so good, but the hiking is fine. Good wide sidewalks lie on both sides of Alaska Avenue and run all the four and one half miles to Wheaton. From there on, even the hiker is pretty much on his own. Then, there is the Rockville Suburban Transportation Company. It appears to be about the most unprosperous transportation company in existence. But this may not be so, as they seemingly have little expense. Riding with the Rockville Suburban Transportation Company however has certain compensations. It can be amusing. It is seldom, if ever, an eventful trip. And if one can relax and resign himself to accept what the Lord provideth, he will eventually reach his destination. It is necessary, of course, to have a flexible schedule. The beginning point for a trip from the District Line to Wheaton is fifty or sixty feet up the street from the DC Transit System's debarking point. It is in front of a hot dog and coffee carry-out stand. Sometimes there will be two, even three buses waiting, contentedly rumbling, chattering, gurgling. Warming up for the run. On the other hand, they may be running only on account that the driver doesn't dare switch off the motor. After all, it might not start again and what one has, one has. The buses are old. They are very old. Most buses their age were junked in 1946, after the war.

A friend of mine recently had what might be termed "a typical beginning." Three buses were waiting. It is presumed they wait for a load to gather. She got into the first one since its motor was running and it was quite filled with passengers. It seemed ready. It soon was. The driver closed the door, engaged the clutch, and stalled the motor. It wouldn't start. The driver kept trying, but, nevertheless, opened the door. To the experienced rider, this meant, get out and get in the next one. My friend did this. This one, too, was now ready. The motor had a fine sounding permanent-like hum. But, since he couldn't go forward because of the stalled bus in front, he shouted to the driver in back to please back up a little. The back driver called out that he would be pleased to oblige, but that he couldn't because he was driving Number 12. Number 12 doesn't have a working reverse. The drivers all got out and held a conference. Some of the riders relaxed. Some of them didn't. Two of the quick decision types got out and engaged the taxis across the street. The drivers decided to move the first bus forward manually. The bumpers didn't match, so the second bus couldn't push the first one. Some passenger help was recruited and the first bus was pushed forward a bit. Driver and passengers loaded up again and pulled out into the traffic, Wheaton bound.

Except for the driver's cheering wave to a stalled comrade near Sennervy Road, the trip was without incident.

Eating Chicken at Home

Mac with sisters, Frances Hulett and Virginia Hall

The other day my oldest sister and her family came up for the day. We were all eating dinner at my mother's home. We were having fried chicken. During the course of the meal my sister remarked that she never knew a chicken had a liver until after she had left home. Our mother always ate it before the chicken got to the table.

And the other day, I remembered that I never tasted the wishbone part of the breast until I left home. My baby sister always got that piece. I don't remember anyone ever saying anything about it. She just got it. Had an unquestioned right to it. No one dared select that choice morsel when the platter passes around.

I can't figure out now why no one ever challenged her right to it.

Eulogy for Jake Boehs

Jake Boehs and Mac Davis

January 7, 1995

I knew Jake Boehs for about seventy years. I knew his father, Ben, and I have faint memories of his grandfather. They were our neighbors. I remember the respect my father had for the three of them. I know Jake and Sally's children. I know their grandchildren.

I look upon the Boehs family as a prime example that decency, honor, and good neighborliness can abide and endure generation upon generation.

When I got to be six years old, my mother took me to the door of that little one-room schoolhouse called Progressive where all eight grades were taught in one room. She introduced me to the teacher, told me to behave myself, and left. I looked around the room with all those great big kids and the question in my mind had nothing to do with behaving myself. My question was, "Am I going to survive?" Jake Boehs was a fourth or fifth grader, and when I saw his familiar face, I was comforted.

We grew up and went our separate ways. In 1961, I moved back to this country, and we got reacquainted through our mutual interest in wheat farming both here in Major County, Oklahoma, and also in Eastern Colorado. He harvested our wheat.

Over the course of thirty-two years, we traveled the roads to Colorado many, many times. He was a great guy to travel with. He had a wry sense of humor. He was a fine storyteller and a mighty good listener.

One time, someone else was riding with us and after six or seven hours of listening to us, asked, "With all this traveling back and forth, do you guys ever tell each other the same old stories?"

And Jake said, "I suspect we do, but we are really polite with each other—we never let on if we have heard the story before."

Both of us were veterans of World War II. Sometimes we talked about that experience. Not about the violence and the horror and the bad stuff.

We talked about funny things, the strange, absurd things. He told me this: "One time I was on a troop train moving across the country and the train stopped on a siding late at night to let another train go by. Another fellow and I stepped out on the platform between the cars to get some fresh air and look around. We were stopped on a street intersection and were looking up the main street of a little town with two dim streetlights. The wind was blowing sand and tumbleweeds and straight trash toward us. The guy with me said, 'Can you imagine anyone voluntarily living in a place like this? It looks like a nightmare!!'

"You know," Jake continued, "That was Eads, Colorado, and three years later, I was living here in Eads working from daylight until dark breaking out the prairie sod trying to make a wheat field, and I've been coming back here for more than forty years."

One time I asked him why he was so partial to Hereford cattle. He kind of hesitated and finally he said, "I guess it was my Grandpa's idea. Grandpa lived about a mile away, and I used to walk over there to watch him feed his bucket calves. One day, I was petting a red and white calf, and my grandfather came over and tied a little rope around its neck. He handed me the rope and said, "Here. Take it home. It's yours. That's a Hereford and they are the best. I was about nine years old, and I don't know how I managed to get that calf home, but I did. I've been raising Herefords ever since because, don't you see, they're the best!"

You and I know how Jake got the calf home. He just kept at it until he got there.

People liked him. In Eads, when he walked into the restaurant of the Co-op, he was welcomed with jokes and banter. If you farm in Kiowa County but don't actually live there year round, they call you a "suitcase farmer." Jake always referred to his long-time friends our there as "the natives."

One time, we pulled into Eads and stopped at the gas station. He knew everybody, of course, so when the operator came out, Jake said, "Hi, Fisher. How's it going out here?" And Fisher replied, "Well, if we could get an inch of rain, we would be in good shape." Jake turned to me and said "You hear that, Mac? You can come to Eads 10,000 times and the first thing the natives here will say is "One inch of rain and we'll be in good shape—out here, they never give up hope."

He liked people. He always had time for kids. In harvest time, it pleased him to give the little kids rides in the combine. Every kid in my family, even second cousins living in Tulsa, made a few trips around the field in the combine with Jake.

Over the years, he had lots of hired hands—old and young. He had the patience to train a young high school boy, and also had an unusual high tolerance for the occasional eccentric that hired on. Bud Boehs once told me, "I think Jake hires some of these characters just to lighten up the scene around here."

He was easy going. As the young folks say, he was laid back. He didn't complain. He didn't make excuses. He didn't go back on his word. He did what he said he would do.

He didn't swear or use bad language. He didn't rant or rave or lay blame. Because, don't you see? That kind of behavior doesn't help anything. Nothing gets done.

He took adversity in stride. Broken down machinery and trucks stuck in muddy fields never seemed to fluster him much. He just set to work doing what had to be done to fix it up or get it going again.

The two most important things in Jake's life were his family and his wheat fields. He was proud of his family. He was proud of their cohesiveness. He was pleased with the way they worked together. He understood their different personalities, and he made allowances for those differences. He was not a man who openly displayed sentimental feelings. He didn't go around slapping backs and giving pep talks. At harvest time, in fact, he might sometimes be—well—grumpy.

But when the combines were all rolling, and the trucks were moving the wheat to the granaries, when all the family was working together, then he was obviously a happy man. He might even fumble around under the seat and come up with a two-year-old package of King Edward's cigars. He seldom lit the cigar. He toyed with it—making fun on himself for being so content and satisfied.

A couple of years ago, Kay and I were out there in Colorado at harvest time. We ate lunch in the field with the crew. Sally and Kathy brought out the lunch. Cindy had gone to town for parts. Bruce, Randall, Gary, Brock, Jake, and Cousin Sam Boehs were running combines and trucks. Jared and Jordan were moving here and there in a pickup. Sometimes, they were running errands, and other times they were—well—learning to drive. Brigit, I think, was back at the house cleaning up the kitchen, and Sherry and Tessa were in Fairview holding down the fort there. I don't know where Johnnie was. Wherever he was, he was busy. Now, that was a family operation if there ever was one.

We are here today to celebrate the life of Jake Boehs. His life with Sally, his life with the family and the wheat fields is a thing to be celebrated. The memory of it all—the effects of it—will endure down through the generations of Boehs. I am grateful for having witnessed it. I have benefited from that life. My family has benefited from that life. I think we have all benefited.

Farming and Poker

The youngest of my children, Jess, has just told me he has decided he will be a farmer.

This surprised me quite a bit. I am forty-eight years old, and he is ten years old.

I have never propagandized him to any line of endeavor. In fact, my observations of the past two years have led me to believe he would choose to be an astronaut, mechanic, birdwatcher, or race car driver. And, if called upon to put my money down, I would have put it on the race car driver line.

A farmer.

"But," he said, "the first piece of machinery I want…" My mind blinked through air-cooled cabbed tractors and red pickups with radio equipment.

Wrong!

"We need an airplane," he said.

So, okay, that is not so wild, but also it is not very practical for our set up—or so I thought.

"Why?"

"So we can go to Hawaii real fast as soon as the wheat is planted," he said.

Not a bad idea thinks me to me. "Okay, Chappio, good night. First we get land."

To choose to be a farmer in this country at this time, to choose this line of effort at the age of ten! To do that, to decide that at the age of ten indicates that his mind is totally unwound and disconnected—or that he is a natural-born, rabid gambler.

He has never shown any signs of disconnectedness, and he has always been sly with his money—allowances, gifts, bottle calves, 4-H pigs, and all of that.

I really think he would gather more gold if he would study the science of poker and dice, but it seems unlikely that he will do that.

Well. And so.

I am a pretty good farmer. I am a fairly good poker player. I know the odds of dice. Don't shoot, toss, throw, or rattle them unless you back the bank. Don't play against the table, in other words.

It is all simple arithmetic. Study before you play. Don't panic (be afraid) when you lose.

Reading and Observing/Free Time

I don't care much for television programs. I'm tone deaf and most taped music jangles my nerves. Thirty minutes of radio is about all I can absorb in one day; so I spend most of my spare time reading, talking, or looking.

In my line of work, there is often no one to talk to except myself—and that gets boring, so I spend a lot of time either reading or just looking. Reading and looking around are pretty much the same thing.

About 90 percent of what I've read has not served me in any useful way and looking around wheat fields in all their various conditions for the past 150 years may have tempered my wisdom, but it has not brought me much knowledge. As one old farmer told me, "What you learn one year can make a fool out of you the next."

Oddities in my reading or looking attract my attention. Here are a few I came across today:

1. Australia, Canada, and Argentina have increased their wheat production fifty percent in the last decade.
2. There is a guy in Spruce Creek, Pennsylvania, who has been studying and photographing the activities of a

certain wild trout fish for four summers. The fish is now thirteen inches long.
3. There is three cents worth of corn in a box of Post Toasties.
4. The Alaska Railroad still makes unscheduled stops to let passengers get off whenever they want to get off. Twenty three such stops on their 356-mile run is the record.
5. I saw a hawk catch a dove on the wing today. I've seen them try it many times, but I never saw a successful attack until today.
6. Aaron Turk will sell you random-size hunks of good steel for twenty cents a pound, which isn't a bad price if he has what you need.

Gift Giving: Books

Kay Davis and youngest grandchild, Becca

Here is what I do: I give books—but I read them first. Two pleasures for the price of one. I have already enjoyed what I am giving away. Never give anyone a bad book.

How can you be sure it's a good book? Read it first. It is the only decent way to do it.

I also like to get books as presents, but I don't trust other people's judgment about what a good book is, so I resort to trickery. Whenever I discover a book I want, I write a note to myself reminding myself to buy such and such a book. Then I leave the note in some carefully selected place where an affluent relative will find it. I fix it up so that the poor relatives have a chance to buy me cheaper books.

This practice has served me well for many years and although everyone is not interested in books, the basic principle of my method could be used for any material thing that interests a person. Merry Christmas!

Note: This list, written on the back of an envelope, appeared in various locations, at different times, throughout the house prior to one Christmas.

Books by B. Traven

The Death Ship
The Cotton Pickers
The Treasure of the Sierra Madre
The Bridge in the Jungle
The White Rose
The Carretta
The March to Caobaland
The Rebellion of the Hanged
General from the Jungle
Stories by the Man Nobody Knows
Night Visitor and Other Stories

Thoughts on Grain Production

Whenever you have a farmer say he wishes the government would just get the hell out of the farm business and let us shift for ourselves, you can be certain you are listening to a person who does not understand either governments or the reality of his life's work.

Governments have been involved in the grain trade and specifically the trading of wheat for at least four hundred years. They aren't going to get out of it. If you think our present day wheat program is complicated, get out the old encyclopedia and read about the English Common Laws Henry VI introduced into England in 1436. And if that doesn't wear you out, go ahead and read about the ones introduced in 1660 or 1791.

Long before Moses struggled up the slope of Mount Sinai where the Lord laid then ten commandments on him, governments were regulating the sale and production of wheat. It is not going to change. There will be a government wheat program of some kind or another for 1986.

The benefits of the 1986 program will not accrue to the producer (the benefits will not clear away many bad Federal Land Bank loans). The benefits fall to the government. Which is why governments have always been involved in the production and trading of grain.

The reason for this is a desire for cheap food. The leaders in any government, in all governments, whether it be a democracy, a dictatorship, a kingdom, or the chiefdom of a Pygmy tribe in the Congo jungles, all harbor one common anxiety, and that is, of course, revolution. What happens if the people revolt?

The most basic human dissatisfaction is hunger. So the basic manipulation of government is to figure out a way to keep the people fed. And the cheaper, the better.

In this country, we raise about three times as much wheat as we can eat. Wheat is cheap. Actually, under the present situation, it seems to me that some farmers are drawing on their savings so they can pay the trucking costs to get the stuff hauled out of the field and off the farm.

Jerry's Pumpkin Patch

March 22 1985

Last spring, a friend came to my house with a quart can of seeds and a proposition. He wanted to plant a valuable crop and was equipped with all the necessities for the project except a suitable patch of ground.

"What sort of seeds has thou in the can, good friend?" I asked. Turned out to be a very special kind of pumpkin seed. He said they were special. To me they looked pretty much like every other pumpkin seed I've looked at.

He wanted to plant at least an acre, maybe two or three, if the seeds held out.

Wheat farmers today do most of their fieldwork sitting on an upholstered adjustable seat in an air-conditioned tractor cab. Melon farmers walk frequently in the hot sun swinging a hoe and carrying a five-gallon can full of bug killer. They also spend a lot of time hunkered in amongst the foliage straightening out tangled vines and focusing fragile blossoms to the sunlight. I prefer wheat.

But he is a good friend, so I agreed to prepare the ground and help load the ripe pumpkins if I can borrow a front-end loader for my tractor, and he could do the rest.

Observations: Locals from Other Countries

Not long ago, my neighbor sent his bulldozer over to dig a big pit for me. Manual, a gentleman from Mexico, who lives up the road with his family, was the driver. Manual's English is a little sketchy, but we got along just fine.

That afternoon, I went into the composing room of the *Fairview Republican* where four people were setting type and laying the next edition of the paper. At that moment, the most vocal person there was Kim, a lady from Vietnam. She was wanting an exact reason why some writer used the word "basics" in a story rather than "basis."

I didn't tell her so, but it sounded like she had already passed by me in the field of grammar. Later that same afternoon, driving north out of town, I noticed the manager of the motel, an East Indian born in Africa, mowing the lawn of his motel. His motel sits at the corner of my first wheat field.

These three contacts with people in our community from other lands and cultures caused me to remark to myself that the community is changing.

Maize

I broke even at the races today and I sure as hell need the money. My rent's due tomorrow.

—Mike Geary/O. J. Leary, 1959

I inspected my maize patch last week, and it is sorry. It has been a dry summer. I don't know why I planted the stuff in the first place. This is wheat country. Maize just works out once in awhile. For me, it was just a kind of experimental crop.

Whenever a farmer plants a new kind of crop or a new variety of seed and it doesn't work out, he can sometimes console himself by telling himself that, after all, it was just an experiment.

Anyway, I inspected the maize and concluded that we could probably harvest enough grain from it to offset the expenses of planting it in the first place. That made me feel pretty good.

Walking back to the pickup, I remembered Mike Geary.

Mike was a man possessed of an obsession. He believed that he could study the history of eight or ten race horses, and on any given day, and predict which one would run the fastest. He was so confident of his ability to do this that he willingly, eagerly bet his money on his judgment.

Although he had a good job as a union printer, he lived frugally. He did not believe in blowing his money for frivolous things. He lived in the back room of a cheap hotel and subsisted mostly on hamburgers and candy bars. His dress was modest. Fifteen years after the war, he still wore his old army overcoat on chilly days.

At one time, he had a wife and some children, but they had left him years before to seek their fortunes elsewhere.

"She insisted on regular meals," was all he ever said about her.

He was kind of a financial wizard, managing at one time to have eight loans floating through nine different loan companies.

"You must always have one of them paid up," he said.

It was a complicated business and I never understood how he did it, but I often thought he could have had a brilliant career in the banking business. He could easily have qualified as a government economist. Geary spent all of his spare time studying the racing news and thick books on the genealogy of horses. He could talk on any subject, but not for long. With him, every topic of conversation soon led back to race horses. He was not satisfied to bet on one race and win. His goal was to bet all races and win all races.

I have not heard from O.J. for twenty years and have no idea what became of him. Perhaps, he hit the big time and now bets thousands where he used to bet twenties. Or maybe, he is in some poor place betting match sticks and peanuts. Wherever he is, he is betting on the races.

As long as I can get hold of a handful of dirt, I suppose I will be sprouting seeds. They will be wheat seeds. No more maize for me. I am not going to get hooked with some stupid obsession like O. J. Geary and bet on a different horse every go around.

Miscellaneous Thoughts

Giving Gifts

When I was a little kid, my Sunday school teacher tried to convince me one Christmas season that it is better to give than it is to receive. My progress in the field of theology very nearly came to a stop.

The Past

When my grandmother ran this farm, she, at one time, had sixteen workhorses, half a dozen milk cows, a couple of hundred hens, two dogs, and a cat named Bluebell. All of the horses, cows, and dogs had names, but the chickens did not.

Farming

One of the reasons for the agricultural success of this country rests in the fact that the men have always worked with the women. This, to a large extent, has not, and does not, occur in the rest of the world—not in the past and not in the present.

Travel

I'm not a good traveler—can't lock (have trouble) the motel door, can't figure out how to use the telephone or the coke machine. The paper machines take my money, and I don't get a paper.

Unsolicited Mail

I don't know how many farm magazines, newspapers, journals, newsletters, fertilizer solicitations I get in the mail every week, but I can tell you, it is a big stack. I don't subscribe to one tenth of them. They come free—gratis. Throughout the year, an avalanche of the above fills up the mailbox.

My Old Dog

March 22, 1985

Of all the hundreds of thousands of species of life on this planet, the only one that mankind has drawn even slightly into his way of thinking is the dog.

I miss my old dog. I miss him like I miss my father and brother who have passed on out of this life.

Once in awhile, my mind malfunctions, the neurons misfire, and I glance round the yards and corral to see what that brown dog is up to now. I do that, and in half a second, it comes to me that he is dead. The engine of my mind whips back onto its proper track.

Once in awhile when I am working in the fields, I have caught myself gazing up the dusty, vacant road wondering if isn't about time for the old man to tootle by in his old blue pickup. The idea hangs a millisecond. Then reality takes command of my brain.

Motocross Racing: A Father's Perspective

Mac with son, Jess, and daughter, Tanya

Mac and Jess

October 24, 1976

First, you have to understand that this is not only the first time, but also probably the last time that I will write down details of a Moto-X race.

To begin with, I was not even supposed to go to this thing. Betty Wallace was supposed to take them. Jess and Tom, that is. Then last night while I was fluffing my pillows, anticipating my first long morning sleep-in since way back there in the summer gone by, the phone rings. Betty Wallace. Unexpected developments. She can't go.

Kay also can't go.

Turns out, finally, that I volunteer to go. The whole deal reminded me of the old army thing, "I need two volunteers, you and you."

I had no choice really. The truck was loaded. The goodie boxes were packed with chicken and cake and Gatorade. The lads were practically beside themselves with excitement.

I went to bed whimpering. The last words I heard were, "And don't forget, we gotta go early. It's 120 miles to the track."

Morning came quickly. It didn't take long to sleep all night. By my second cup of coffee I even worked up a little enthusiasm. Away we go to the Wallace's. It is chilly morning. We are met by Betty and her three boys. It is her truck we are going in. She gives me endless instructions about the truck. I finally tell her to go back to bed. I can drive a pick-up truck.

Off we go, four abreast in the seat. Kid brother Kurt somehow or another has waggled into the deal. (Unbeknownst to us, he had smuggled himself in the back of the truck, but that's another story.)

I will not go into what paraphernalia is needed to run two cycles in a Moto-X race, but I can tell you the whole truck was full. Back end and front end.

The pleasant smell of new fried chicken fills the cab. By the end of the adventure, the smells of gasoline, castor oil, fish oil, and God knows what other things are used in motorcycle engines will have dulled the sense of smell to uselessness.

We drive to Ponca City. It is cold. Dodge pick-ups leak cold air around the doors. The sky is purple blue. Remindful of blizzards. The boys chatter incessantly. Their talk is full of bikers' jargon and motor technicalities. I sit mute. I give lots of attention to driving.

We get to the track. It is real first class, organized Moto-X track. No hacked out deal in some pasture. A real track! First one any of us have ever seen.

The boys get the registration and the fee thing settled. Naturally, it costs about twenty dollars more than anyone expected. At a first class track, man, you have got to be registered with the AMA and so forth and so on.

We get into the pits. A glorified name for a spot on the hillside grass where you just park and unload your gear and get ready. There are several score of outfits carrying from one to four cycles. We are not a very flashy outfit. In fact, we probably look a little seedy. My boys haven't seventy-five dollar boots and no leathers, the padded racing pants. But they have good bikes and good helmets and farmer boy boots.

Moto-X races run according to class and size of bike. Class goes according to experience, the amount of winning you have done in the past. It is ranked: #1 Novice, #2 Amateur, #3 Expert.

We run novice.

The size of the bike goes according to the cubic centimeter displacement of the engine's piston and generally is defined as 100 cc, 125 cc, 250 cc, and open, which means anything above 250 cc. Tom is running 125 cc and Jess is running 250 cc.

So, the afternoon events go thus: 100 cc Novice, 100 cc Amateur, 100 cc Expert, and so on through the whole thing.

Once in awhile, they throw in a little warmer-upper race. For instance, a "Powder-Puff" race, for girls only. I understand that it is losing popularity now, any girl who is serious about racing is not going to be put of into a for-girls-only thing. Today's warmer-upper is a "no class, no size limit, open to anybody who has never won a trophy on this track." It is three times around, and that's it.

Jess and seven other guys enter. The gate drops and off they roar and damned if he doesn't come in second! We are only twenty minutes into a long afternoon and we have got a sure-nuff, guaranteed trophy!

Then the long grind begins. Each race runs several laps. Each class runs twice. In other words, they run the whole show twice. The way you average out in the two heats is how you place in the race.

Finally, Jess's class comes up. Fifteen entries. Crowded.

They go, and I see that he got a good start—about fourth or fifth on the way to the first turn.

You can't tell anything at that turn. Too many things going on. They are all into it at one time. The second turn is about thirty yards beyond. I get a glimpse of him on the way to the second turn. He made it through the melee. When they clear the second turn, he is running second. They run four laps. He stays in second for three and a half laps, and man, oh, man, it is a fast thing with lots of jumps and slides. In the middle of the last lap, he cuts the number one bike off at a sharp turn and he is in the lead. He turns on all the juice and crosses the finish about forty yards in front. Made it look easy.

He lazes it back to our pit spot. He rips off the helmet, the goggles, and the chin guard. The temperature is about forty degrees, but his face is covered with sweat, and he seems to have more teeth than Jimmy Carter.

"That was the most fun I ever had!" he said.

I can't think of anything profound to say, so I just say, "Yeah, man!" And then he starts getting it ready for the next run which is two hours away.

To make the story of a long day short, Jess runs number one in the next race—twenty-five entries. An ominous lineup I can tell you. I calculate $30,000 worth of gear sitting in line waiting for the gate to drop.

My chap looks pretty poor, except for the bike, which is not the fanciest, nor the costliest out there, but it is a long way from a heap of junk. His uniform is dreary. He is still wearing GI boots that really look like they were there. And just before the race, he splits his jeans from stem to stern. We patch that up with a long yardage of duct tape, and I keep assuring him that nothing is hanging out and that will probably suffer nothing but a cold butt.

On the second heat, he gets a really bad start and goes into the first turn about fifteenth. On the second turn, he comes out running seventh. On the next lap around, damn if he isn't running number two. I do not know how he passed five machines in one lap. Anyway, he did, and he comes in number two for the heat, which gives him first place for the race.

Home at dark, we have the trophies sitting on the piano, and they look real nice.

Musical Talents

No one recognized our sister Frances's musical talents sooner than she did herself. At the age of five, she helped enthusiastically with the hymn singing in church. She sometimes practiced them on the way home from church.

Her tone, rhythm, and tune were flawless as I recall, but she butchered up the lyrics in an awful and artful way.

We were coming home one Sunday in the 1926 Dodge sedan which was a wonderful car for hauling around kids. The back seat was roomy.

Frances was standing up looking out the side window, singing "Rescue the Perishing."

About the third time, she started through this fine old hymn, Mama turned around grinning and said, "Wait a minute, Frances, wait a minute! It's 'rescue the perishing,' not 'Rex chewed the parafin.'"

Musings on Burial Practices

January 16, 1970

There are no laws or instructions for me as to what I should do with a dead cow. I can tow one of my 1,200 pound dead cows onto any far corner of my farm I want to for the coyotes and vultures, the worms, and nature. There exists no law to deny me this right. No one questions my right to do this. Almost no one would say I had not done the best thing under the circumstances. Should I dare to do this to a deceased relation, I'm sure that I would find myself in great legal troubles, and I might even be classified as a nut, a ne'er do well, and a man of no substance. It is pretty certain if I willed my dead remains to be treated in such a manner, they wouldn't be. It is likely that the state of Oklahoma will request that my body be indigestibly embalmed and buried at a safe depth of six or seven feet.

Burial practices are immoral on the basis that they deny nature of some of its true feeding. When bodies are embalmed and buried to a depth of six or seven feet, their physical usability has become nil. Most of the social laws regarding the burial of humans are based upon a peculiarly motivated proposition. It is an idea fundamentally based on man's civilization and religiosity, assuming that religiosity is a thing learned and acknowledging that civilization is also a thing learned. It is not logical to put sterilized corpses deep into the ground. Such a custom benefits no life on this earth. A corpse upon the ground free to the air and worms of the soil will benefit the earth more. All life feeds on some other life, be it live or dead. A true civilization should make such food available to those things that need it.

Thoughts on Death

Life is an accidental incident. Death is an incidental absolute. (July 1970)

July 1971

Death is a thing most people fear. They fear it so much that down through the centuries and countless generations of mankind, myths have evolved and religions have developed filled with philosophies organized to ease one's life from now to the hereafter.

Now is now and death is nothing. It is not a thing to be feared, and life is not a thing to be regretted.

The world swung before I got here. It will swing when I am not here. I do not wish I had born in the times of, say, Columbus, or Eric the Red. It also eases me to know that I will not be the forty-ninth person to stroll around on the moon.

In short, I am where I am. I do not regret being born later than I was. I will not regret dying earlier than I think necessary. I have come into life and I will go out of it. No one thing is more understandable than the other.

Musings on Farming

As a general rule, I have found that the most useless and time-wasting thing a farmer can do is talk about farm economics. In the first place, very few folks outside the farming business can understand what you are talking about, and in the second place, those folks that do understand what you are talking about figure you are lying. Those folks in the farming business who, of course, understand what you are talking about will listen out of politeness, but they are just waiting for an opening because they know damn well they can explain the situation better than you can anyway.

Every farm paper and magazine you pick up has countless articles by spokesmen of scores of farm organizations and associations and commissions and state university extension departments, all telling each other over and over the same sad stories. I have read the same OSU extension story in as many as five different farm publications. Nine times out of ten when a farm story does somehow drift into a general type of publication, the statistical figures will be jumbled out of place and the decimals will be in such a way as to make the whole writing a senseless and meaningless drivel. The only thing that ever filters out to the general public is, "Man, them farmers sure deal in big numbers. That must be the reason groceries are so high," and the words tons, bushels, and acres are incomprehensible to the average citizen.

But they all do know that tons, bushels, and acres are something they don't and couldn't lift. "Them farmers get so much and I have trouble paying for just one little sack of groceries."

Devil Lanes

"Devil Lanes" are not common anymore, and, in fact, not many people are familiar with the term. They still exist in this country, mostly as a result of laziness or economics.

Once they existed as monuments to the civilized rights of one man to disagree with his neighbors.

I am talking about fences.

The early day custom developed, and still exists, that the fence between two farms should rest on the following basis of responsibility:

Each owner should face the proposed boundary to be fenced from a station on his own land. The half of the boundary to his left was his responsibility.

Simple enough— assuming everybody agrees on the boundary line—which goes from *this* point to *that* point. The remarkable thing about the first settlers is that they did understand where *this* point and *that* point actually was—a great tribute to the 1873 government land surveyors who measured out this land and marked the section corners with stones, charcoal, and cedar stakes.

But back to the Devil Lanes. In the early days, when the first fences were set up, disputes of boundaries did arise.

A natural human problem. After all, the original surveys were made twenty to twenty-five years before the need for fences arrived. Some of the markers were gone, and some people didn't measure distances with the same precision as did his neighbor. One man stepped it off; his neighbor used a tape.

Disagreement, naturally, came about occasionally. How to solve it?

They came up with Devil's Lane idea.

"I'll move back one rod and build my fence, and to hell with you."

So, the space in between came to be known as "Devil's Lane."

It isn't done anymore. The land is too valuable for that solution. So, when disputes arise, we go back to the surveyor and ask him to establish the line. The dispute is settled.

I Could Have Been a Wayward Son

Mac's Dad, Fred Davis

1986

Standing with my father in a field of ripening wheat, I watched him gaze, with obvious satisfaction, to the north, to the south, and, finally, west toward the setting sun.

"It's good," he said. "Real good."

It was his sixtieth crop. He plucked one head of the grain, rubbed the kernels out in his palm, tongued them to his teeth, and tested the hardness.

"Be ready Tuesday," he said, "if the weather holds."

Once again he gazed across the vast field in all directions.

"It's good land. It's good land, and you've done a good job."

Then without any lead-in or introduction, he told me this story.

"When I was fourteen, Mama sent me to town one morning with a letter for old man Bower, the banker.

'We're going to borrow fifty dollars,' she said. 'We can repay him when we thresh the wheat. I have explained it all to him here in this letter. And here is a list of goods we need. Get that at Wedel's grocery.'

I put the saddle on Dolly, mama's buggy mare. She was the nicest horse we had, and I rode into town.

Old Bower read the letter, scratched his ear, smoothed his mustache, and finally opened his desk drawer and handed me two dollars. 'Go get your groceries,' he said, 'while I fix up the papers.'

When I got back from the store, Bower was standing in front of his office looking at the sky.

"The weather's going to change," he said, "you'll need to move along. That's a real nice mare. Does she ride easy? Here's the money."

He counted it out, "Four eagles, a five dollar piece, three silver dollars, and the two dollars I have already given you. Here is the mortgage note. Tell your mother to sign right here on this line. You three sons sign right here as witnesses on these three lines, oldest first. That's Jacob, isn't it? Then you sign here and have Dawson sign the last line. Tell your mother to put it in the mail box first thing in the morning. That way I'll have it back here in time to record it before the courthouse closes. Now hurry along, the wind's coming up."

About a mile out of town, I stopped to count the money and look at the note. It excited me to suddenly realize that I held the money in my hand and that the note was worthless until it was signed. I rode on. Dolly had a smooth and easy gait. Temptation bored in on me. Maybe it was time to seek my fortune elsewhere. If I just kept going south, I could be in Canton by sundown. I could be in Texas by Monday. I could be in California within six weeks, easy on this good mare. Or I could sell the mare and take a train, I could be in Los Angeles in less than a week. I could get a job on a ship. I could be in China by Thanksgiving. I could be all over the world by my sixteenth birthday.

Dolly slowed to a walk when we clattered across Sand Creek. Time to decide. Ride south toward Canton or turn east toward home.

Guilt and Christianity struck. Mama would need the mare Sunday for the buggy. Mama was a teetotaling, hymn singing, 100 percent Methodist. We helped to build the church for heaven's sake. Old man Bower would accuse me of fraud, chicanery, deceit, robbery! The neighbors would call me wayward...and mean to boot...to steal the banker's gold and run away with his widowed mother's only buggy horse.

Dolly turned east and I let her. I kicked her in the ribs and loped on home."

With that, my old man turned and looked across the field again.

"Yep," he grinned. "It could have been different. I could have been a wayward son."

Notes on Hats

On a head-high row of pegs to the right of the door are the hats. The everyday-using hats, three felts, two straws. The good hat, the 5X beaver is not there. It is in the closet, on the top shelf, in a round hatbox with the leather-backed clothes brush on top, weighing down the lid.

The hats on the pegs are old hats—battered, creased, even crumpled. The side brims curl up, some more than others. The front brims on all of them snap low down so that the head must tip back for long views, which gives a heightened air of alertness and inquisitiveness to the wearer.

When my friend, this horseman, this cowboy, this anachronism leaves his house, he selects a hat, one of the five. The selection appears to hinge on the weather and the upcoming action. If he is not going into the weather, if he is going to church or the rodeo, or taking his wife out for supper, he will, of course, already be wearing the 5X beaver when he gets to the door. He goes to rodeos as a spectator. The roping days are over—except, of course, at home where the working days are not over.

Notes on the Road

July 2, 1972

So we are out in Boise City, Oklahoma, a town at the western end of the Oklahoma panhandle. Beautiful country. No wider, more isolated, cultivated country exists in the world. You can drive for miles and never see signs of human habitation—never see movement—seldom even see a tractor, yet, all around is cultivated ground and well-fenced pastures. Signs that someone appears long enough to put things in order.

We drove from Guymon to Boise City, and, mostly, we observed the sky, which sometimes comes down all around us—a sky full of fleecy clouds and thunderheads—the billowy kind.

Six, seven, eight miles east of Boise City, the car thunked. Stop to peek under the hood. The fan is not fanning, the belts are not turning. In fact, they looked like three dead snakes draped over the fan and all. Go on to Boise City. Fast. Thinking any second the motor will heat up tight and stop.

Stop at the first station on the outskirts of Boise. The sign says, "Fulltime Mechanic." They don't even have a part-time mechanic.

The kid on duty says, "I don't know anything about mechanics, but it looks to me like you done ruined the motor."

Think, think, Pontiac motors, costs umpteen hundred dollars, takes dozens of days to order, get, and install. Shot down in Boise City, I think.

But the world turns up the friendliest, most helpful people when you least expect it. I am standing there contemplating this mess on a hot afternoon in the western reaches of the Panhandle of Oklahoma, and my mind is grappling with how to get on down the road, and I'm thinking about how do you buy a car or pickup (new or used) in a strange town two hundred miles from home base. How do you do the money thing and all that? What do you do with a heap of iron setting on the filling-station man's drive?

Miracle!

Peanut man flashes in the other drive. You know, hearty sort, driving a van type thing full of ten-cent packages of peanuts. His job is servicing peanut machines in the Oklahoma panhandle, parts of Texas, Kansas, Colorado, and New Mexico.

Later, he told me, "I hit the road twenty hours a day, five days a week."

"You must work on a commission basis," was the only thing I could think to say.

At any rate, he examined my smoldering heap of junk.

"Hop in," he said, "I'll move the peanuts and clear a way for your bags. I see that Allen is still open. He can fix the motor, and if we hurry, you can still get a room at the Star Motel."

So we unloaded the car and literally dumped off Kay and Jess and the luggage at the Star Motel and hurried on down to see Allen, who was just closing up the shop (8:00 p.m.). The peanut man tells his mechanic friend what the problem is. He includes the information that wife and kid have been dumped at the nearest motel.

"It is likely they won't get a room," said the mechanic to the peanut man.

"They fill up early," he added.

The peanut man said, "This man is in trouble. You can fix him up." So the mechanic went to telephone and called a buddy who operated an independent shop.

After one or two minutes of kidding around about some guy having something screwed off, they arranged to put my car in operation "about ten in the morning."

The peanut man hauled me back to the motel and went on about his hundred mile run. He told me his name was Bill. I forgot his last name.

Outlaws

Dick Yaeger and Isaac Black were a couple of early days Oklahoma outlaws who spent quite a bit of their short lives roaming around Major County. Black had relatives here and seems to have been locally known as just another young fellow that got started down the wrong path in life. Yaeger was a little older and more experienced in the robbing business, supposedly having loped along with the Doolin gang of bad guys over in eastern and central Oklahoma. Perhaps, Black did too. No one today knows for sure. People involved in that line of work had little sense of history. They seldom kept diaries or wrote letters which anyone thought worth keeping.

Black and Yaeger activities in Major County seem mostly to have revolved around their immediate need for fresh horses and/or a solid meal. There are numerous accounts in our county history of these chaps "borrowing" saddle horses and some wife to serve them a good meal.

Sometimes, they returned the horses and sometimes they paid for the meals.

Outlaws are by no means a bygone way of life. They are still with us. By the 1890s, however, outlaws on horseback were out of step with the changing times. Black and Yaeger ended their careers like most outlaws of that time—young, bloody, and dead.

The big posses that hunted them down became relentless and were frequently replenished with rented horses and eager citizens.

Isaac Black was shot and killed in a cornfield near Longdale. Days later, Dick Yaeger was shot and captured near Hennessy.

Black's body was hauled that night to the county seat in Alva. He lies buried in the Alva Municipal Cemetery.

List of Our Pets and Other Animals

Fuzzy the Cat
Queenie: The hunter, killer of rats, snakes, mice, rabbits, traveled all day, out thought rabbits and Brownie
Simon Kling Hammer Head
Fluffy: Poodle
Brownie: Lazy yard dog, run over by a rabbit
Poochie: The rambling stud, part-time fighter
Patrick: Mother
Pepper
Porky
Salamanders: Laid eggs
Snakes: Hognose from Marguerite W.
Chameleon
White mice
Brown Dog
Big Orange
Misty
Peaty the Sparrow
Three-legged jack rabbit
Misty: Deaf cat
Dawg
White dog with ten pups given to the Indians
Tadpoles
Fairy shrimp
Porky the Racoon
Preying Mantis
Seahorses
Quinto
Siamese Fighting Fish

Return to Fairview, Oklahoma, 1962

After eighteen years, I've returned to my spawning grounds and it is fine to be back amidst the slightly changed scenery of childhood and youth to meet new relations and old friends and acquaintances. People remember the most peculiar and astonishing things of little significance at the time—and by me, long forgotten.

    I stopped at the liquor store to make a modest purchase and while chatting with the lady behind the counter (she looked vaguely familiar), two slightly loaded jaspers breeze in and give me a big hello.

    "Hi, hi. Why, Mac, my old drinking buddy! How have you been? Where have you been? Getting a little juice, huh. Remember the trip we made to Nebraska for seed…barley…remember? Big red truck…and you shooting pheasants as we drove down the road. Have you still got that little Belgian gun? Oh my!"

    To the others, he said, "We were drinking quite a bit and I got to feeling bad, so we stopped, and I bought a bottle of Peppermint Schnapps and I drank some of that and we ate a steak dinner… remember that steak, Mac? And then I felt real good. That Peppermint Schnapps is what did it, made me feel good."

    Later I remembered this happened fifteen years earlier when I was on a two-week furlough home.

Photograph of the Ancestors

In the interest of accuracy, precision, and exactness, I journeyed out to the cemetery yesterday to check the dates on my grandma Lisethe's tombstone. July 5, 1873 is what it reads. I recall Uncle Jake saying one time, in the course of a conversation about turkey eggs and bull snakes that Mama was born shortly after the Civil War.

I tell you this so you will see that oral history and folklore and so forth are really just as historically accurate, precise, and exact as any documented and pinned down research might be. Looking back over 130 years of the past, you would have to admit that Uncle Jake's timing of Grandma's birth as "shortly after the Civil War" is precise, accurate, and exact.

Another reason for telling you about my journey to the cemetery is to let you know that this short plunge into the realms of historical research has freed my mind considerably. It has lubricated the process of this project. No more research and documentation will be necessary. I just need to remember what I saw and what I heard and the facts will be right at hand.

The stone that marks my grandmother's grave also marks the grave of my grandfather, William Davis. Born December 3, 1871; died April 20, 1906. A short life of thirty five years. A short active life. He left three sons aged ten, eight, and six. His widowed wife was thirty-three years old. He left them living in a two story house, which he had just finished building some months earlier. The house sat on his proved-up homestead of 160 acres in the Cherokee Strip in Oklahoma.

There are two photographs of William Davis. In one he stands with his wife on their wedding day, April 13, 1892. They are dressed to the nines. They are gussied up. They are in a studio looking straight into the camera lens. Not smiling, not grim. Stalwart and determined is how they look. In the other picture of William Davis, he is again standing with his wife. Between them stand three small boys about three, five, and seven years old. The children are dressed in what surely must be their best clothes, their Sunday clothes. The adults are plainly dressed. The group stands in front of a sod house. A hut, a house made of earth. Near the house stand a team of horses at rest. The faces are not clearly in focus. They stand more or less at attention. It is an important event. They are having a picture, their picture, made.

These two pictures have hung on the walls of this house for ninety years. Five generations have passed back and forth before the pictures. Occasionally a visitor notices them. To the rest of us they are unremarkable, part of the house, like a cupboard drawer.

Reminiscing

1980s

After I took the treatment, as they say, and became a better person, I had an awful lot of time on my hands, which I had heretofore never been burdened with.

Up until that time a normal day was about one fifth or four six-packs long, depending upon my inclination and circumstances.

It came slowly to my mind, but quickly became a tiresome reality, that your average better type person looks upon a day as being twenty-four hours long.

So, okay, to fit into the scheme of the warp and woof around the stable, well-adjusted standard citizenry, one works for seven or eight hours, spends forty-five minutes taking on fuel for the body and kills about one hour washing teeth, combing hair and sorting socks. What then?

After all, how much meditating, postulating, and psychic adjustment can one handle in a day. Being quick witted and in good health, I can take on a full load in thirty second intervals. Which is the way I do it. No use to overload the mental circuits.

That left me with thirteen hours for sleeping and whatever, which is definitely way too much for a sane and well adjusted person like myself.

I cast around for options, and was advised by what appeared to be normal people, to take up some activity such as jogging or stamp collecting. These, and simpler type suggestions did not fit into the realm of reality upon which I embarked.

I decided to become a cattleman, a cowboy, a keeper of livestock, a producer of meat. It is simple enough. Cows have calves. Calves grow up, get fat, are butchered, and, ergo, steaks. Who doesn't like steaks?

Another Rooster Story

Yesterday, our rooster began crowing at 4:37 a.m. It is not often that I am aware of the life around me at that time of day, but yesterday was an exception. The rooster crowed loudly and vigorously every ten minutes for the next hour and a half while I lay snug and cozy, reading in bed.

There is no legitimate reason for anybody (other than milkmen and cops) to be awake at four thirty in the morning. I was awake because the crowing rooster woke me and kept me awake.

It was comforting and satisfying to hear him sound off in such a regular and exuberant manner. A few months ago, he was a ragged, sad-eyed, stress-ridden specimen of chicken food, with no tail feathers. Today, I am confident he would be judged champion chicken in any poultry show in the world. Viewed here at his own farm today in all his splendor, anyone with any quick judgment at all can readily see that he is an extraordinary bird. A creature above other creatures. Dogs, cats, cows, small children, and sensible adults are aware of his presence from forty yards away.

He draws all attention by his perfect rooster appearance and demeanor, and he commands respect by eye contact. When he looks at you, first with one eye and then the other, you know instinctively, intuitively, and absolutely, that you are confronting a positive force in first-class condition. Like the dog and the cat and the small children, I am perfectly content to go about my business and let him strut about his.

How did this rooster move up in the world from lowly status to an admirable status? I can tell you. He lost his competition and became his natural self. Our chicken flock originated with two roosters and eighteen hens, all mature, pure bred, brown leghorns. Within a matter of weeks, and despite their perfect accommodations and high dollar feed, it was the most dejected and dilapidated bunch of birds you can imagine. All of them lost their tail feathers. Their eyes glazed over, and they became flighty and apparently demented. It was a distressing situation.

Then one day, a friend, who didn't know much about chickens, came by and said, "I need some chickens. Where can I get a few chickens?"

"Good friend," I said, "you have come to the right place. We have more than we need. Take half these chickens, and God bless you."

It is terrible how we sometimes take advantage of our friends. I wanted to give him all of the chickens, but I was afraid he might get suspicious and think something was wrong with them. We gathered up and caged nine hens and one rooster, and he went home happy as a kid with a new bike.

Unfortunately, real disaster struck his flock. Within a week, he was out of the chicken business. They were eaten by a raccoon.

We were lucky, however. Our flock underwent a miraculous turn around. The chickens all developed elegant tails. The feathers took on a glossy sheen and their eyes began to sparkle. The rooster had become a firm but loving and benevolent dictator. The hens cluck softly and stroll about with obvious contentment and serenity. The refrigerator is full of eggs, and, all in all, it is probably the most perfect ten bird flock of chickens the world has ever known.

Stock Man

1971

A true stock man's sense of security rests not in the number of his cattle not in the price of his beef on the market. Security descends upon the true stock man when he is absolutely certain he has readily accessible to the cattle far more feed than the cattle can eat. Exultation comes when he sits in a warm house on a blizzard day and looks out through a double-pane window upon his cattle feeding and resting in dry shelter. It is then that the idea comes to him: "I surely sit in the favored hand of God."

Sunday Night Poker Games

The Sunday night poker game begins about 7 p.m. We sit up to a commercially designed poker table with collapsible legs, like a card table. If we crowd up, eight people can play. There is a little pit for the money and indent for the coffee cup at each place. Seven usually play, but we have room for one visitor—eight players, of course, limit the game we can play—can't play draw with eight. Not with this group, anyway.

We play penny-ante-ten-cent limit. No big deal. We troop in with our money bags. I carry mine in a blue nylon sock. Melvin carries his in a green Mason jar. He says the jar is worth more than the money. Two old ladies use a velvet Crown Royal bag with a golden draw string. One skinny old boy carries his in his front pocket. He wears tight jeans and it makes a big lump on his thigh. He usually spills a handful while transferring the money from his pocket to the table. We are pretty casual about the money. Several years ago, everyone counted out the money before we started. We kept the pennies and nickels and the dimes neatly stacked, or at least separated into piles. When the game was over, 10 p.m. sharp, we carefully, maybe courteously, counted the money into the bags, jars, and cans, whatever. Some announced their winnings or losing. Some kept their standing secret.

Customs and habits change. Now, everyone bellies up to the table and pours a cupful or so of coins into the little pit, sets the bag on the floor, and we begin. When the game is over, we pour our coins back into the bag of the bag and estimate the win or loss by the heft of the bag. "Feels like a two buck gain," one says. Another assays his by the size of the money bag, "This sock looked like it was holding a grapefruit when I came in here, now it looks like a lemon…you wizards have me down about 400 cents."

Whoever folds away the table usually picks up ten to fifteen pennies from the floor. The rule is she has to keep them.

We play dealer's choice with a few restrictions. No goofy games with wild cards, no spit-in-the-ocean, or baseball, or such absurdities. We do play with one joker, which plays with aces, straights, or flushes. It is fully wild in low-ball hands. The problem with the joker took about a year to resolve. Mr. Hoyle's book of rules for poker ignores even the consideration of the joker— at least, my edition does. We are a mature, tolerant, reasonable group, and after forty-two more or less vigorous discussions, we solved the problem by vote. Fortunately, we voted when seven, not eight, players were present, and we voted four to three to do it the way we do it. Although it is a nuisance (the joker), you get used to it after a few months and seldom think about it, except when someone beats out your three eights with two aces and a joker.

Talking to Inanimate Objects: Lawnmowers

I am getting a little ticked off at the chauvinism of people who tout the beneficial results obtained by talking to philodendrons and petunias. They completely ignore the really practical and truly helpful effects that come about by talking to such so-called inanimate objects as TV sets, lawn mowers, and balky automobiles.

Is there one person in these United States who has not brought a misbehaving TV into proper focus with a sharp rap and a mumbled threat? Of course not. Mechanically inept suburbanites have successfully been kicking and cursing power mowers into humming submission for almost a generation now. There are meek automobile engines scattered all over the northern states that respond satisfactorily on cold mornings to a sound starter—stomping and light cursing.

My point is simply that there is a far more effective approach than all this rapping, threatening, kicking, cussing, stomping, and cursing business. Yes, indeed. A gentle, persuasive tone is needed. A comradely tone if you will.

My TV set has so much empathy for me that a mere wave of my hand and the briefest of coaxing bring it into sharp focus.

I approach my lawn mower machine as I would an old friend. Something like, "Well, old buddy, shall we take few turns around the south forty this evening?" Works almost every time. It starts on the first heave of the rope.

My car is getting old. Its carburetor and breathing apparatus is clogged and wheezy. It sputters and coughs. It hacks and belches. It stutters. It runs. I know that my supportive encouragement is the only thing that keeps it functioning. I talk to that car like my wife did to me on our honeymoon.

Well, that takes a big irksome burden off my chest.

Tending Cats

Cat and Mouse drawing

I have been batching for the past few days, and I have discovered that one of the most intricate chores around the household is attending to the cat.

I can manage the washing machine and the skillet and things like that, but that cat is something else. People have three basic attitudes towards cats. They love them, hate, them, or tolerate them. I am a *tolerator*.

I wouldn't go out of my way to kick a cat; and I would pat one that sat down beside me and purred. At the same time, I expect a cat to show some gratefulness when I feed it. My wife's cat does not.

Even when Ms. Prima Donna is eating one of the three foods she does eat, she is disdainful. She nibbles at her food for a few seconds. Then she stares at the wall for a while and grooms her ears. It takes her thirty minutes to eat two ounces of ground fish heads. I like an animal to eat with gusto. My old dog can devour two pounds of anything in eight seconds. And he wags his tail and moans with happiness doing it.

Cats are creatures of habit, and ours is no exception. She has a morning resting place, an afternoon resting place, and an evening resting place. At night, she goes out. I don't know where she goes, but I suppose she goes to rest somewhere.

The Blizzard Story

Februrary 24, 1971

So Sunday, we wake up to a winter wonderland; the beginning of a blizzard which by midmorning was in such a rage as to make the farm invisible.

Jesse's comment on snow Monday, "Daddy, this must be the only place it snows horizontally instead of vertically."

This went on into Monday evening, which found us deadlocked by various drifts around and about the place, ranging up to eight feet deep in one place near the cow shed and in half a dozen other places, five feet.

The catastrophe of it all began Sunday afternoon when I realized that it wasn't going to let up, and we wouldn't be able to get hay and water over to the West 80 where we have (had) forty-four cattle. They just drifted away with the blizzard. They did.

This morning, I got a report of where a third little bunch of them are. Now, when I can get to the three places where people tell me some of my cattle are, maybe I can count them.

Tuesday morning, calm, bright. Get a tractor going—2:00 p.m. got a tractor going—impossible to get out to the road. With Kay's help, dug through a big drift, drove into wheat field, wandered around for awhile, and finally came out some place near Aunt Emma's.

After blazing a trail with the tractor to the school house, came back, tied on pickup and water wagon, loaded up wife and kids and hay. Started for West 80. A needless trip, since the place was vacant of cattle. Got back to highway, sent Kay and kids on to town with grandparents for supplies and water tank. Kay sent Tanya and Jesse into store while she and Grandpa had weird experiences with packing the water wagon. Tanya and Jesse lost list so bought only neccessities: four bottles of catsup, two packages of cookies, ice cream, six cans of cat food, two pizza mixes, some candy, and one bar of soap. Forgot meat, milk, bread, toilet paper, and matches, etc, etc.

While waiting at school corner, I accepted free high class shot of booze from passing deacon of local church.

Monday morning, during driving blizzard, Jesse and papa rush to a snowdrift near the cedar trees to midwife a calf from an extraordinarily forlorn mama. We used the chain and block and tackle, tied to a tree. We heaved the giant baby, all slithering, out onto the snowdrift birth bed. Mama cow got up and did her thing, and Jesse and papa slithered back to house, leaving cow, calf, block, tackle, and chain to the elements. Later on, carried calf into shed from which, of course, it soon came right back to its lowing mama.

Nature is fantastic, not to mention unbelievable, even when you observe closely. The calf is now sixty hours old, big, fat, and frisky. Gives no more thought to snowdrifts than spring calves do to lush, grassy meadows. And mama, on her snowdrift, is so contented with the state of affairs that she amiably tolerated the children's petting while she munches the oats they carry out to her two times a day.

Cal footed in a carton of cigarettes Monday evening, bless his soul.

Wednesday morning up at five thirty—by God! Ready for the day's onslaught. Insisted Kay fry eggs for me. After six cups of coffee, nine telephone calls and a curt briefing to my now-back-in-bed wife (none of which she remembered, it proved, as the day wore on), I hopped onto my now smoothly functioning tractor and wandered away amidst the snow drifts and on up to Progressive Corner. There, I had, with great foresight, parked my trusty, almost-never-fail, twenty-year-old pickup the night before. The mission was exact and simple. I was on to the tip, the track, the trail of the third bunch of drifted away cattle. My blood was up. I was hot on the trail.

The day was ticking away like clockwork.

Ten minutes later, it was 7:45 a.m. I was two and a half miles from home, hopelessly stuck in a snowdrift, pacing homeward at a steady 130 steps to the minute.

Well, so, unplanned events occur, chin up. The noble soul goes ever onward. Plan the next move and get to it. Back to the tractor, back to the house, rouse out Kay, get her suited, give instructions to the kinder and get back to the snows, trails, and roads to haul out the stuck truck. Cold-ass ride for half-awake, slightly bewildered and put-upon wife.

Got it all out and back home easy as pie.

Approximately 900 episodes, or action ideas, or moments of truth, one might say, occurred until the end of the working day.

From then on, it was all, however, left-handed, cross-eyed, pigeon toed, and tongue tied.

Several times during the day, the thought came to me that heart failure from pure physical strain would be next. Once, the now-awful thought, came to me—I can't express it except to say it had to do with brutish mayhem. Then there was a moment about 3:30 p.m. when I had the really startling thought that if I would just sit down on this snow drift and let myself go, I could melt the whole goddamn thing with tears. It is puzzling to tell you that that thought seemed to cheer me. I picked up de hoe and dem barges and swung dos bales or however it goes.

There were actually only two positive things that happened after the successful pull-the-pickup-out affair, oh so long, long, ago.

The day ended.

In the midst of something, somebody called to announce the happy news that my income tax papers were complete—ready for signatures and affidavits and checks and so forth and so on.

My sweet wife set me down to supper (the hour was a fashionable 8:30 p.m.).

Since then, it has been all coffee and cakes.

But somehow, it seems like I haven't even started with these notes. Someday, maybe I will find the courage, the nerve, to attempt to put them down.

But probably not. I can already feel the mental blackout process going to work.

Thoughts on the Constitution

1960

The Constitution of this country is good. The founding fathers of this country—the youthful, dissenting revolutionaries who wrested this land from the armies of the overlords of England—knew exactly what they were doing when they compiled it.

It is one of the shortest governmental constitutions ever written. It has endured longer than any.

It is being raped by men who yearn for power and money, and the citizens, whom it in theory, protects, are also being raped.

The US Constitution was compiled by intelligent men who were knowledgeable about centuries of governmental abuse upon the common, ordinary, working, loving citizen. They knew what oppression was. Indentured servants, slavery, usury, imprisonment for debt, indenture to the military (draft), invasions of privacy (seizures of bedroom and kitchen goods of private life).

Yes, they knew oppression. They knew what it meant. Most governmental constitutions go to great lengths to outline what the government will do for the people. The US Constitution is unique; it pointedly outlines what the government cannot do to the people. It is on this basis that it has stumbled along more or less for two hundred–odd years.

I think it has now reached its lowest point of influence in the government. I think that's bad, and I think it is time to do something about it. Let us briefly review the Constitution of the United States. Let us see first if there is something wrong with it—let us have clear-minded men propose changes. No single soul there agreed to all of it, but all of us here are ruled by it. If changes are in order, let us make them.

Travel Trailers

Over a period of several years, my wife occasionally brought up the subject of travel trailers. She wanted one. She said it would be fun and a cheap way to go on vacations.

My defense was always the same: I concentrated on the word *cheap*. I would write down the price of the trailer and divide that figure by the going rate for a good motel room. It usually figured out we could spend about a year in a motel for the cost of the trailer.

But you can only work the same defense about so many times before you get outmaneuvered. My cousin's brother-in-law came along one day with a real nice trailer for a very decent price.

We parked it under an elm tree out by the garage and there it sat for two years. The children took it down the road twenty miles to Canton Lake for the weekend a few times, but the only trip I ever made with it was hauling it back on Monday after they were gone.

Last month, my wife and I took a trip in the travel coach. We don't call it a trailer anymore. In one way, it was really an eventful journey, and, in another way, it was slow and leisurely. We went to South Padre Island near Brownsville, Texas. It took us seven days to get there.

When we got there, I remarked that we could have made the trip on horseback in about two weeks.

Hawk Observations

I have watched for three days one single unidentifiable hawk. Tractoring around on my south fields, I have had long, long hours to wait and then watch his return to my part of his range.

This coming back occurs about once an hour from seven in the morning until eight in the evening. He cruises my 240 acres there for about five to ten minutes. I calculated his territory covers about three to five square miles.

His appetite is stupendous. I saw him strike three doves this morning. No knowing how many he struck that I didn't see.

He hits young rabbits and also mice too for a quick three-bite snack.

I have seen the hawk drop like a bomb from nowhere on to a scurrying mouse twenty feet from my tractor.

He clutches the mouse, kills the mouse, flits to a steady perch (clod, fence post, whatever), gulps the mouse in three quick snatches, gets himself airborne in an easy liftoff and is instantly soaring and searching. All this in less than fifteen seconds.

Dove and quail are another story. He misses more than he catches. Dove flight-altitude across stubbled fields varies from two to twenty feet.

The hawk frequently attacks them in flight. His easiest mark, of course, is some twitching thing on the ground. His hunting is all done by sight alone — his endless sweeps across the fields search for movement on the immoveable terrain. Irregular movement (wind movements are cancelled out) means life. Life means food. Ergo, attack!

If the hawk spots, say, a flying dove and decides to attack, he ceases to soar and begins to fly. He flies intently, fast, to catch the dove. As he approaches the dove, a World War I–airplane-dog fight –thing begins. To catch the dove in flight, the hawk has to get his claws on the dove—a very difficult areobatic maneuver, pehaps, impossible. I have seen a hawk catch a dove in flight only once.

When he does succeed with a flying dove, he follows another technique. The hawk is twenty times bigger than the dove. He flies farther. He stays above the dove and badgers it to the ground. Then the hawk has another snack. The dove is an erratic flyer. (*Darty* is a word that a shot-gun hunter of them will use.)

The doves in flight foil the hawk more often than not. But hawks don't count odds, and they hunt almost incessantly. From time to time, however, the hawk comes to earth for nothing more than a brief rest. A great hawk, one of the Buteos, descending to the earth for rest, must surely excel all creatures of this earth for grace and splendor.

When the hawk comes down for brief rest, (it is always brief—five minutes or such), and it soars down to thirty to forty feet above the ground, heads into the wind, sets wings, tail, beak, and pin feathers too for all I know, and floats motionless to earth.

The pefect solid suspended in the absolute space.

It touches the earth like a wisp of fluff and closes its wings without haste, and with a blinkless eye, turns its head and views the scene with a powerful disdain.

Although the big hawks, the Buteos, seem, on casual observations, to be ceaseless hunters, I think sometimes they soar for pure sensational pleasure.

I have seen them suddenly stop their incessant searching and rise on a good thermal with set wings to three thousand feet.

Once up there, they will head into the wind and appear to concentrate on their motionless suspension for minutes on end.

The wind filters through their feathers. What are they doing up there three thousand feet above food and action?

When they hunt, they make their swooping strikes from no more than one hundred foot altitude.

So why do they hang for minutes on end, soaring at three thousand feet?

For no reason at all I think, except that it is surely a pleasant thing to do.

More about Hawks

Hawks of the Buteo family have broad wings and broad rounded tails. The most common species in this area are the red-tailed, the red-shouldered, and the Swainson's. The Swainson's hawk is the one species of Buteo which migrates in flocks. Once we counted over fifty of these great birds resting as they perched on scattered clods in Ed Karber's wheat field. The identification of these different species is difficult and I read that experts of the business say it is sometimes impossible unless you have the bird in hand, which, of course, is seldom the case. In my case, it has never been the case.

Red-tails are the easiest to identify and that's about as far as I go. If the hawk I'm watching has broad wings and a broad tail, it's a Buteo, and that's close enough for my interest.

I have watched these creatures quite a lot because their most favored hunting areas in this part of the country seem to be wheat stubble fields. When a hawk hunts over a field, he searches erratic movement in the stubble—the scurry of a mouse, the flutter of a dove's wings, the awkward hop of a baby rabbit.

Their vision is extraordinary. I do not know what their limits are, but I once saw a red-tail dive from his perch on a power pole, set his wings for a glide, and strike a mouse running in the stubble over five hundred feet away from the power pole. With his belly brushing the stubble, the hawk cupped his wings, brought himself into a vertical position, and dropped one leg to clutch the running mouse in his talons.

It is unusual to see them strike from a perch. Most often they spot their lunch while in flight, and then, depending how far away the target is, and how fast it is moving, the hawk either glides into a strike, or flies rapidly to the target. They strike, of course, with their talons. They grasp their prey and kill it by puncturing it with their talons. The kill has to be quick.

When they are after a rabbit, they sometimes change their mind and pull up from a strike if at the least instant, the rabbit looks too big. A half-grown jackrabbit is too big.

Rabbits kick, and hawks are not interested in combat.

Envelope: Keep

November 1968

It may as well be said from the start that I am what most people would call an alcoholic (although, very few people know it; maybe even, like nobody but me, and, of course, my wife, dear soul). I've been sipping the juice for twenty-nine years.

I was seventeen years old when I got my first drink of real booze. Moonshine whiskey; clear as water, seventy-five cents the pint. It was instant love. I ignored it for fifteen years or so. Then I accepted it for what it was to me: the juice of life. Some people paint pictures to express their life. Some work for money and/or status. Some become wrapped in technology, enthralled even. Like flying around the moon. Some go into politics, the dumbest thing of all things. Barbaric. Not even that. Savage, would better apply. A prostitution of the mind.

I've tried them all, except politics, of course, and none of them suited me. Fit me out, I mean, and tied me to life and the stuff that is now.

The stuff that is now along with me. The stuff and thing that will go along after me with my kith and kin; with my children, blessed, beautiful things; with my cattle and my bulls, poor creatures; and the vigorous, silent wheat seed that grows in all my fields and rests also quietly in my granaries. And the trees I know, many have I planted and seven I helped to plant now stand fifty feet or more into the air. When I was a kid, I daily hauled water in cans and poured it around them and thus sustained their life. Now they comfort me. In summer, they shade the relentless sun. In winter, they give body to the bleakness of the sky. I have not planted a tree for quite some time. The last trees I planted were cedar.

My old grandmother plants a tree every year. I used to think that peculiar. She is well into her eighties. In fact, she is almost to the ninetieth year of life, and the trees she planted in her seventies give her much pleasure. And so it goes. I guess I've got a thing with trees. But my mind is small. They grab me as individuals but a forest bewilders me.

Why I Farm

Mac back at the farm, 1940s

At the supper table one evening, I delivered myself of a long monologue on the trials and tribulations I had endured throughout a long day of exceptional adversity. I closed this depressing tirade with the remark that farming is an activity similar to alcoholism and drug addiction.

It is something a man just gets into and then can't get loose from. My wife said, "Well." She said it again. "Well," she said, "would you say the wife of such a man is a fool or a saint?" Then she said, "We have some chocolate cake and homemade ice cream for dessert. Have you got enough strength left to handle some of that?"

Over the years of farming, my reasons for farming have varied. At one time, I would have said I farmed because I wanted the independence and creative fulfillment it brings, that farm life is the best way to raise a family. In good years, it even looks like a money-making proposition.

For multitudes of people trudging daily to jobs they don't care much about, farming is an enviable way of life. It looks so serene, so tranquil, so casual—so free.

When the work is all done, when the farmer has done all he can do to create the right environment for crops and cattle to grow and reproduce, when he is coasting, so to speak, waiting for God and nature to once again reveal the annual miracle of growth and reproduction, then it is indeed time for tranquility, serenity, and, yes, casualness.

Mac and Kay Davis at home

Now that I am retired and spend my days philosophizing and, occasionally, jockeying a tractor around the field for my son (if it's all hooked up and everything is working right), I can look back and say it is an enviable life. I experienced all those good things and, too, I am now kind of proud that with the help of a wise, humorous wife and her chocolate cakes, I was able to transcend the days of adversity.

Belize Adventures

Introduction to Belize

At the beach in Belize

Mac's nephew, Skip White, became intrigued with Belize, Central America by reading a *National Geographic* article. In the early 1970s, Mac, Skip, Ed King, and Dave Lowry traveled by car to Belize and fell in love with the beauty of Belize. Four families purchased a small ocean-front lot near the village of Placencia. Skip and his family returned to build a dome house on the lot. Several years later Skip and his family returned to Belize, bought adjoining property and built a resort, which was known as the

Turtle Inn. It included a home for themselves and huts which were rented to guests. Mac and Kay and many family members enjoyed numerous and memorable visits to Belize throughout the years.

Belize (Notes from a Farmer 1982)

If you look at a map of Central America, you will find a little country just south of Mexico, on the coast of the Caribbean Sea, named British Honduras. If the map is new, the country is named Belize.

It is about nine times the size of Major County and is unique in many ways. It lies north to south about one hundred and sixty miles long and fifty miles wide. It has coastlands, swamplands, jungles, uplands, and mountains. Rainfall varies from fifty inches in the north to one hundred and sixty inches in the south. It is sparsely populated, somewhere between 100,000 and 150,000, depending on who is making the estimate. To a farmer, it looks vastly undeveloped.

On the other hand, after visiting the place three different times, I am beginning to think maybe it just looks undeveloped because I don't understand the system. No one is starving, no one is fussing, no one is begging. No one, absolutely no one, is in a hurry; except, of course, the occasional tourist passing through. Everyone wears clean clothes. Belizean ladies seem to enjoy scrubbing clothes and hanging out the laundry. The common language is English. The education system and the system of government is derived from England. England and Spain squabbled over the territory back in the seventeenth century. England won.

And that, I think, is what makes Belize so much different from the rest of Latin America. Great Britain and the Anglican Church shaped the culture.

A hodge-podge of ethnic groups makes up the Belizean people. I read somewhere that about sixty percent of the population is of African descent and Afro-European descent and that the remained is made up of Mayan, Mestizo, Afro-Caribe, European, Asian, and East Indian as well as all the mixtures that have occurred among them in infinite variety. That about covers it, except to mention the Chinese folk who run the Golden Dragon restaurant in Belize City.

Belize accepted its independence from England last September. They have been talking about it for twenty years. Some wanted it, and some didn't. Belize has no army. It has a very low-profile police force. The British army maintains a presence there, but it too, is low-key.

Central America is much in the news these days, and it is difficult to understand what is going on in places like El Salvador and Nicaragua. Down in Belize, things may change, but for right now, it is easy going and all laid back, as the young folk say.

By George, I just remembered! There is no television down there either. It's wonderful.

Journey to Belize

We didn't draw lots. I can't honestly tell you if I was hustling for the prime position or just trying to be benevolent. Instinct and experience blend to shade our reasoning.

I volunteered (perhaps, I demanded) to ride first in back, in the camper shell, and let the three young bloods ride forward in the cab on the first part of the journey through Oklahoma and Texas.

So off we go at 7 a.m. on a Saturday morning with the loved ones kissing and waving us away. And I flake out on the pad in the back and don't wake up until we are a long way into Texas.

I remembered the war years and the endless movement in "personnel carriers" through back roads in Texas and Virginia and England and France and Germany, and I remembered the best way to go is supine and in sleep. Of course, you miss a lot of scenery in that state, so you condition yourself to rouse up and be alert when you pass through some unfamiliar land.

In Texas, we had a meal in a Mexican restaurant and the feeling comes upon me that we are moving into another culture. The people are more relaxed. The women look different.

At this point in the story, I should tell you that like the main character in Rudyard Kipling's story, *The Man Who Would Be King*, I took a vow to myself that I would ignore all invitations to ladies and booze—reserving of course, beer, which would allow or permit me to visit all places where ladies and booze are about.

Journey to Placentia, Belize

Nov 30, 1988

It is now fifteen days since we drove away from Aunt Fran's door. We have been here since Wednesday night, the only time we drove at night on the entire trip which was 2,264 miles from our place. It is 4 p.m., and we are having what can only be called a downpour. The house appears to be leak free. By standing on the bed, I can see through one of the dozens of lookout ports the top of the water reservoir, sealed across the top, except for a square foot screened opening into which three gutter pipes are pouring water into the tanks for our fresh water supply.

When we arrived here I was beginning to feel the bad effects of a couple of Mexican lunches that would have gagged a buzzard, and by Thanksgiving evening, I was laid up, or, at least, laid out and did not enjoy much of anything for two or three days. Now I am in pretty good shape and Kay is stretched out (struck her yesterday), pondering the true meaning of life. She is down, but I know she'll be fine in a day or so. At noon, we had chicken soup and cheddar cheese which seemed like a nice change from shrimp and the finest fish in the world. Shrimp (big ones) are two US dollars per pound here and you would be surprised how common tasting a food they can become if you eat them three days in a row.

The trip through Mexico was interesting and beautiful but stressful because of the roads, which aren't bad but just require constant watchfulness on account of the narrowness and plenty of traffic. Mexican bus drivers and truck drivers are scarcely the world's best. Really! What they do is a kind of elaborate Moto-X driving. We never saw any wrecks or fender bashing although that looked inevitable every minute of the drive. In the rural areas where we were most of the time, there seemed to be millions of people everywhere—except in the dryer regions. In the southern part, in the mountains and rolling countryside, in the wet and fertile area, there are always people walking or working along the roadside. I don't know where they all live. We would roll through what looked like a village in a valley, and a sign on the roadside stated "25,000 inhabitants," and seven or eight miles down the road, another village, posted "30,000 inhabitants."

One night we stayed in a beautiful place about twenty miles off the road named Palenque, near the most elaborate of Mayan ruins. We toured the ruins the next day and stayed another night. It was inexpensive by US terms at about thirty dollars a night for a very fine room and twelve dollars for the best meals for both of us. We were tired and it was a fine rest stop.

Coming into Belize in late afternoon, we had unexpected trouble with the vehicle and did not get away for sixteen hours. I mean we left everything and took a bus to Corozal for the night. Went back the next morning and paid the bandits $1200 duty on the vehicle (78% tax). Of course, Skipper will pick that up on the title change, but still it was a lot more than anyone expected.

The last twenty miles here on "the new road" was about equal to a Major County section line road in need of grading, but the thirty miles before that were bad, bad, bad. It was along here that Kay (who, by the way, drove every mile of the way) picked up a hitch-hiker, a Mayan lady with a three-month old baby. She spoke English and was talkative and open. She had been visiting her sister in the country who was in distress.

"She have eight children and her mon in de jail since las week they pick 'im up for carryin' five stone a da weed."

We let the lady out at the foot of a timbered mountain, which she said she lived at the top of. Kay gave her a satchel for her bags and parcels and our best flashlight.

Later when I started to chide her about the flashlight, Kay cut me down pretty sharp, "What better thing could you do with a flashlight than give it to a poor woman getting ready to climb a mountain in the middle of a dark night with a three-month old baby and thirty pounds of stuff."

Right, of course, and I haven't missed the flashlight, not even once.

Chris and Skip have really done a lot of work here and have a really nice place with 300 feet of beach all neat and clean for 150 feet back from the water. The last time we were here, it was just bush. It looks like they are making a success of this. Right now they have twelve guests who will leave next Sunday after two weeks here. They are connected to the organization *Earthwatch* and can go out mucking around in the lagoon all day counting insects and dead leaves. They pay a pretty penny for the privilege. The leader of the group will be back in a week with another group for two more weeks.

Skip and Chris have four or five people working around there. They set out high quality meals, which, believe me, is rare in this end of the world. We ate Thanksgiving with them and it was fine.

The mail goes out tomorrow! Have been in the sea four times, but it is a little cool now.

Love, love, Papa

Belize Trip

Wednesday, December 11, 12, or 13, 1988

Yesterday, we went to Dangriga by bus. A trip to Dangriga by bus begins early. It is a fifty-four-mile trip one way and takes about two and a half hours—one way. At 5:30 a.m., we locked the door, started for the road fifty yards away. We hear the bus. The bus goes by. We shout, whistle, wave our arms, the bus stops, backs up. We get on. So far, six passengers. Next stop, Seine Bight—unless someone steps out of the bush and waves. At Seine Bight, we take on eighteen to twenty passengers. The conductor slaps in a new tape and we rollick away—a Christmas carol with a steel-drum reggae beat. The one amplifier is up front, and the volume is carefully adjusted so that all can hear. It is an older school bus from the states—pretty good condition. The driver is very careful. The road is dirt, in need of grading. He weaves through the potholes. He uses all the road. There is no traffic. The passengers are cheerful, teasing, in a good mood. Most of the ladies are big and dressed like Aunt Jemima. Two or three girls are dressed to please the eye. There are three or four babies. A Mayan family gets on, and the bus is now full—everybody clean and neat. One middle-aged guy takes a clothes brush out of his bag and brushes his hat. He is the only person with a hat. Everyone else carries at least one bag. The guy with the hat seems to have nothing in his shopping bag but the brush. The driver is wearing a navy blue tam—militarist, for some reason, scraggly bearded, a T-shirt, red sweat pants, and tennis shoes with no laces. We stopped two times to "fullup" the radiator. The conductor stands by the open door—a smallish guy, except for his cap which is the same style as fifty million farmers wear. The logo had script writing, which I never noticed. Kay says it reads: When you're flat on your ass, everybody wants a piece of your ass.

Halfway to Dangriga, he works his way up the aisle taking the fares—seven dollars, Belize.

It takes quite awhile, because now, the bus is loaded—some standing in the aisle. A little sign at the front of the bus says "Capacity 66." I figured out it is sixty-six if twelve are standing. The conductor seems to have an assistant—more or less—he helps load on the people and the bags and the babies, and he also raised the hood when it was fullup time. The conductor seems to be in charge, but a sign above the driver says the driver is in charge. Actually, Ms. Cherry was in charge. Ms. Cherry sat behind the driver and, as I learned later, is an employee of the lady who mortgaged her home and little store to buy the bus when they made the road to Placencia a couple of years ago. I think she serves as a presence-of-management, goodwill hostess or something. Chris reminds the conductor to gather in the fares, "fullup" the radiator, and stay on schedule. A cheerful, good-natured lady.

On the return trip, it turns out that the assistant conductor is the return trip driver. Too strenuous a drive for one guy to do both ways. He was a big, black guy with a limp, and a militaristic bearing on account of his seriousness and the fact that he wore what looked like army fatigues, including a camouflage floppy cloth hat that hung over his ears and neck.

Dangriga is at the mouth of Stann Creek Valley where the Stann Creek River empties into the sea. The valley has many orange groves. The oranges are processed into juice concentrate and shipped out to the world in barrels and tanks. Dangriga is a village of 20,000 with many small shops, Chinese restaurants, and people wandering here and there. Blacks, Creole, Maya, Chinese, some whites, and all combinations of the above. The sidewalks, where they exist, are board—old boards, and the drainage is mostly open. The stores and shops are organized like stores were in Isabella and the other small towns in the twenties and thirties. The manager is behind a counter and his goods are close at hand in bins, on shelves, or hanging from poles and hooks in the ceiling.

We went into (or, at least, looked into) most of them. Kay bought a Guatamalan skirt and a pair of flip-flops. I bought a machete with a tooled leather scabbard and a bag of peanuts from a vendor. We sat on the river bank, and I dozed in the sun. We crossed the bridge three or four times, stood on the bridge, and looked at the river and the boats and the coconut trees. The same fried-brain Jamaican guy hit me twice for "a cigarette, mon." There were three beggars in town; an old, old man with one leg and a forked tree limb for a crutch, an ancient black woman with a dirty crumpled note that stated she was a Honduran refugee with no children, no man, and that she suffered from heart disease and homesickness.

When the Jamaican hit me up the second time, I reminded him we had met an hour ago at the other end of the street. "Ah, yes," he said, "I am a travelin' man. I bin all over Central America." As far as I know, he made it through the rest of the day with no more help from me. We ate lobster in a Chinese restaurant. We walked three-quarters of a mile along a street running parallel and three hundred feet from the sea.

The land between the street and the sea was vacant and upon this grassy expanse were tethered twelve horses and one heifer. All looked as though they needed a pill or shot of some kind—not Class A stock. Quaint—a sort of antique pastoral scene. The sea, the green grass, the horses, the street with no cars, nobody but us, the row of houses—some ramshackle, some neat—quiet—Siesta time. At twelve, the stores close up—except for the restaurants. At two, they all open up again.

At three o'clock, the bus loads up and we go home. Music all the way. We get home in the dark. For the last hour on the the trip, Kay holds a tiny two-year old girl while the mother across the aisle dozes. Kay talks to the child—still fairly neat and clean after the all day trip—hair ribbons and bows still in place. Kay feeds her cookies and counts her toes and lets her play with a pen and paper. The child smiles and looks and listens and never utters a sound. Finally, she just goes to sleep. And the music hammers on. When a tape played out, another one was going in four or five seconds. The driver or the conductor was always ready to zip out the old and punch in the new—like maybe the tape had something to do with how the bus functioned as a whole. A couple of times when they snatched out the played-out cartridge, the tape would hang up, and yards of the stuff would swirl around the driver and the conductor. After the new tape was in and rolling, the conductor gathered up the loops and swirls and carefully rolled it all back in the cartridge with a pencil stuck in the sprocket hole. All this while standing by the open door with the bus weaving and bouncing through the potholes. Once he dropped the tape to grab hold and save himself from sailing out into the bush. Someone else grabbed the tape and so all was saved.

Baking Bread in Belize

Notes from a Farmer, February 11, 1982

In the fishing village of Placentia on the west coast of the Caribbean, you cannot buy bread in either one of the two grocery stores. If you want bread, you must make arrangements with the local bakers, Ms. Cooncoo and Ms. Lily.

Also, you must order the bread the day before you need it. These ladies have got their business down to a fine point. Each day's supply is sold before it is baked. No waste, no storage, no wrapper, cash in hand, and you take your loaf right off the cooling rack.

My interest was drawn to this business when I learned their only capital outlay was the cost of flour and yeast. The flour is milled from wheat shipped from the port of Galveston.

Since most of Major County's wheat is exported through Galveston, I imagined myself watching my own wheat being baked into bread in the village of Placentia.

The whole business takes place out in the backyard under the coconut trees. The dough mixing goes on behind a windbreak of corrugated tin and palm fronds (to ward off the sea breeze from the rising dough). The tables are makeshift, and the pans are of odd shapes and sizes.

The dough is made with unbleached wheat flour, coconut milk, coconut oil, and a little yeast and salt. When the dough is ready, it is shaped into round loaves and put into the oven.

The oven is made from the bottom twelve inches of a fifty-five-gallon oil drum. It is supported over a coconut husk fire by three tin cans. The top of the oven is a scrap of rusty, smoke-blackened corrugated tin covered with a circle of glowing coals. The fire is tended constantly by one of the bakers. An ever-changing arrangement of the coals seems to be very important.

After a while, the oven is opened and the loaves set out to cool. The bread is dark golden brown, fine textured and a little bit sweet. It is not quite as tasty as my wife's bread, but beats Rainbow and Wonder Bread by a country mile.

Notes from Belize

January 21. Watched a four-man crew load a small pick-up-size load of Coke bottles on a dugout dory equipped with a twenty-five horsepower Yamaha outboard motor. They left for Stann Creek town about thirty-two miles up the coast where they will exchange the empties for full ones and return to the Cozy Corner Entertainment Center (a beach side hangout). It is an all day job for the four men and the boat and the motor. In the Cozy Corner, the cokes will be chilled and served over the bar along with a plastic cup for two bits, US money. No tip will be expected and the music is free, and for all of that, as you can imagine, it takes cheap labor.

Belizean Mechanic's Shop

Mac and W in Belize

November 15, 1992

It is a two-bay garage in the frontyard. A structure with a roof and one wall. The roof is a hodge-podge of corrugated sheet metal, old boards, and old car doors with the glass intact. Concrete pillars hold up the roof. Around the edges of the structure is a bank of old engine blocks and rusty crankshafts.

The floor is concrete covered with a thick layer of hard-packed sand and oil. Next to the working bay is a small wooden building where the delicate work on generators and starters is done. Against one wall are the bench and vise. A path leads from the door to the bench. The rest of the floor is covered with a two-foot layer of discarded armatures, starters, brackets, and hanks of wiring—all rusted and mossy.

Everything looks as though it has been there for half a century—except the hand tools, burnished with use.

Hanging from one of the pillars by a strand of kinked and rusted wire is a faded, greasy sign, which reads:

We don give credits.
The management of this garage
We don lend tools
We sell tools—we rent tools.

Letter from the Dome House, Placentia, Belize

Belize (Mac with nephew, Skip, and Jess)

November 6, 1992. 11:08 a.m.

We are here and everything looks very nice—about two acres of clean swept beach with here and there a palm tree and big bushes in bloom with red and yellow flowers—and an orchid blooming on the side of a tree near the door. We spent most of the morning "going to the store" and the fish house and the post office and helping Skip push a little pickup out of the sand.

Since we were here three years ago, they have built a new post office. It is not an imposing structure and is, in fact, decomposing and rotting way this very minute. It is a little bigger than our wire shed with a tin awning about the same size. Customers stand in the sand under the awning and do business at a counter about chin high. The south side of the building has two windows open to the sea breezes. The mail is tied in bundles and lays around on boxes and crates amongst other bundles not tied but weighted down with coral stones or empty pop bottles. A small bank of pigeon holes hangs on wall, all stuffed with the post office records. The Belizians are strong on making out receipts, the copies of which they stuff into the pigeon holes. The gentle sea breezes keep everything aflutter and occasionally a scrap of paper sails aimlessly through the air. In the interest of efficiency and expedient service, a patron who is a big-mail receiver, such as the Turtle Inn, is allowed to sort through the stacks and bundles while the clerk busies herself searching for the big stuff—newspapers and magazine. She might even ask one of the three or four loiterers sitting under the awning to hand over a magazine he is reading because it belongs to the Turtle Inn. Today, they had no stamps because the girl that does the stamps "is gone today." But it was no big thing. Leave your money and your cards and letters and it will be taken care of.

Wednesday we went to Laughing Bird Caye: a tiny island with fifteen to twenty palm trees, a nice beach, and wonderful coral. We snorkeled with our new masks and fins. The expensive snorkel tubes are worth the money; they work perfectly. Kay's fins are hot pink. Mine are blue and so we make a cute pair of old withered snorkelers. Skip, our guest, and we made the trip (ten miles out on a choppy sea). Kay paddled around over the corals in twenty-five feet of water but still claims she can't swim!

Skip has the place in fine shape and seems to be constantly building and maintaining, so I presume he is making money although he has no guests right now. His latest acquisition is a big compressor machine to fill scuba diving tanks. A fifteen-thousand-dollar rig. It needs its own little house, which they are building.

Everyone works at a snail's pace and people stroll rather than walk, except for an occasional tourist jogger who seems bent on killing himself and the two tall German frauleins who stride by in their skimpies intent on getting somewhere real soon.

Now, it is dark and I bid you bye-bye, we are having lobster tonight.

Love, Mac

Letters from Mac

As mentioned before, Mac was a prolific letter writer, and his letters were eagerly awaited by friends and family. Because his eldest daughter lived abroad for many years, she was the fortunate recipient of hundreds of letters, which even now, are still a delight to share with family. Like the columns, the letters are a collection of stories, insights, and anecdotes.

The first several letters were written to his sister, Frances. Mac was twenty years old and preparing to go to Europe.

Arrival in Camp Swift, Texas February 6, 1943

Dear Sis,

I am now a member of that soon-to-be immortal regiment known as the 146th Engineer Combat Regiment. Sounds romantic, huh? I spent fourteen days at Fort Sill at the reception center and then was moved down here to help make up a new regiment they are forming. There will be about 1500 when they all get here, and I was in the first 300 so I'm going to try my damnedest to get above the pick and shovel grade (at least, I've got good intentions).

I got your letter the other day via Fairview. Certainly was glad to hear from you. I like that quick responsive way you have of answering mail. Seriously, don't you think two months and ten days is a little long to wait for a reply from your own blood sister? Hereafter, try to do better, I demand it of you, don't want to break the morale of the armed forces, do you?

Which brings to mind the heroic soldier home from the battlefront you were telling me about. Who is he, what is he, where is he, why is he, where is he, and he's getting along…I mean, how you are all getting along? Another thing—don't get too many men on the hook, irons in the fire, or whatever you want to call it, sometimes develops into complications they say. Bob's courtship is certainly about to wear me out, it's on, it's off, it's on, it's off, it's on, it's off—reminds you of a lightening bug, doesn't it? I don't know how the hell it will all come out. I don't even think God does, at least he isn't giving us a hint as to the ultimate outcome of this deal. Take G., for example: Last summer, I was the main oarsman. Then I throw my paddle away and get out and swim. Couple or three weeks before I leave, with a little encouragement on her part, I get back in the boat. Before long, I'm pulling all my oars and a week before I leave I become a regular outboard motor. Three or four days before I leave, we get right chummy. She starts talking about getting married and little blond-headed kids running around our house—course, I didn't discourage her. Now what do you think of that?

I got a letter from Virginia the other day. She's getting to be quite a gal, popular and all that stuff. She writes a pretty good letter too. You know, full of little jokes; good, meaty gossip—almost as good as you.

Dad stopped at Fort Sill twice while I was there. He said they hadn't heard from you for a couple of weeks, you ought to be ashamed. Take me, I write at least every other day. Aren't I good? You really should write more often. It's kinda lonesome for them there now.

I better write to Virginia now.

Love and all that rot, (Lil' Abner) Mac.

Shouldn't have put those last four words on, but I'll leave them now. Sorry.

Life in Camp Swift, Texas
Austin 11:45 a.m., Sunday, 1943

Dear Sis,

You'll have to overlook a few minor points of penmanship. Reasons: Number one, the pen I am using is kind of like the ones that lay around on Post Office desks. Number two, I'm not what you could consider at my steadiest point. That's the effect beer has on some people.

At the present setting, I am one of the numerous service clubs situated somewhere around and about this fair city. Right nice place. There is one of the most beautiful ladies here. I would say she is probably fifty or sixty. You can just look at her across the room and see the charm drip off. I bet when she was about twenty-five, she was a killer. Over in one corner, there is a piano trying its damnedest to be heard above the uproar of its accompanists. There is a great big artillery man who must have been in opera. If he wasn't, he should have been. He has a super deep bass voice and is slightly inebriated (phonic spelling), so you can imagine the consequence. He has a pint bottle sticking out of one pocket and one of those "To Mother" kerchief deals sticking out the other. A stub cigar in one hand and wears his pants similar to what L. B. Davis does (Betty Lou's dad). Quite a character. You should hear him give out with "The Volga Boatman." With all the motions and such, it's quite impressive, no doubt about it.

I came to town with a couple of the boys. One is a big, six-foot-four Irishman who can't pronounce his Rs, named O'Hagan, from Nevada. (Such a grammatical construction—Ms. Derryberry would probably sit down and commit hara-kiri or something if she saw that last sentence.)

The other one is a blond-headed kid from Salt Lake. Wears his hair crew style and is a football player.

The weather down here is hot—period. We have been wearing our suntans for the last three weeks. I suppose it is still cool up there. My basic training will be over the 22nd of May and from there it's anybody's guess. I've heard from Dallas Howerton a few times lately, and from what I gather, he is in one of those repair forces that are way back in the bushes. He said he couldn't find his way out if he had to and candles were the source of illumination comes the night. Kenneth K. is in New Caledonia.

I received the book you sent some three or four months ago, and I might say it is a most exacting piece of literature. I thought I told you that in my last letter; but if I never, I never. I'm much obliged for the book. Say, don't you have a birthday soon? Or was it in April? I shouldn't forget things like that.

Again, I beg your pardon of this inexcusable mess. It's just like I said, it's the pen and all. Goodbye now.

Love, Mac.

(*To Frances at a Wash DC address from Dad mailed from Camp Swift TX address while in Indiana*) **Wednesday August 18, 1943**

Mac's sister, Frances

First Report from Indiana

August 18, 1943

Hi Hon,

How is the girl from the short-grass country getting along in the short-grass country? Maybe though, you be getting homesick for the crowds and cheese sandwiches of our nation's capital. I, personally, will be pleased to plant my GIs into the terra firma of Oklahoma again.

With all the nursing experience you seem to be getting, you will be prepared for any eventuality—hmm. Not to change the subject much, but are you still helping to make the postal department a paying thing by keeping a steady flow of correspondence flowing towards Washington? Just as a matter of interest you know.

While I think of it (I'm in the habit of forgetting little things, you know?), I was glad to get the ten bucks—naturally, and I thank you very much for the same, though I didn't really expect or figure on it. Now that you have gone to all the trouble to get it here, I will naturally not bother to send it back merely because I wasn't figuring on it—naturally.

I got a letter (a card) from Bob who is somewhere in South Dakota. He said that as soon as he's got time, he would write me a thesis entitled *Space*. I guess it's kind of barren in Dakota.

The bell just rang (the one that rings about this time every night), and that means that the lights are supposed to be turned out. It's hard for me to write in the dark so I will be quitting any time now.

I shall be looking for the time when I can sit down and write you a letter. You'd better not wait till I do that though, just go ahead and write anyway.

Now, goodnight, my love.
Mac.

PS: You said something about all the time forgetting who you were feuding with. That, my dear, is the mark of a truly gentle woman.

7:30 a.m. the next morning. It's a fine cool morning back here in Indiana, cool, anyway; and morning, that's sure.

Brief Chat September 26, 1944 France

Hi Sister Dear!

Here I am way out in the woods living a life of ease and tranquility. Seems as though it's been quite a spell since I had words from your part of the country- yes indeed, quite a spell.

I had the pleasure of visiting "Paree" sometime ago and that is quite a town, to say the least. It is a very beautiful city. The people are all very friendly and the differences of language proved scarcely any handicap at all. After all, some things are practically universal and with enough motions we can be made to understand most anything and everything.

Is Bill still stationed in Washington? I suppose so. Next time you see them, remember me to them and tell them I'd like to spend Christmas with them, but I just don't believe I can make it. Travel difficulties, don't you know.

About the time I left England, I discovered that I was only about twenty-five miles from your friend. I never got out that way. She probably wouldn't have been home anyway.

Our little sister has been launched upon her college career so I have been told. I bet she has quite a time. She said she had the "sweetest" sister who sent her a beautiful fur coat so she wouldn't be cold at those football games.

I reckon this is about it for now. I trust and hope that you and yours are well, and all of that. I hear a couple of McCues are likewise awaiting a blessed event. That's what makes families.

Love, Mac

Some Impressions of Paris October 27, 1944

Dear Sister (and prospective diaper changer of my first nephew!),

I am practically an uncle! Do I give cigars, or do I get them? I received your letter of the 27th of September, which is exactly one month ago. To say I was glad to hear from you would be somewhat of an understatement. I read your letter and the one I got from Virginia the same day. I can't tell you how I felt, but it was nice! I have two wonderful sisters.

About the packages and books: I haven't yet received any of the ones you sent, not even the peanuts from last July—I fear they would be slightly stale by now. I imagine the packages will start coming soon as everybody seems to have sent me something. I thank you for *The Works of Robert Service*, but as it would be a little inconvenient to carry them around at this particular time, I'll ask you to hold off sending them just now. Perhaps I will become permanently situated sometime, and then I will be glad to have them. I always kinda liked his style of writing—guess it's the wanderlust in me. I still have it— the wanderlust, I mean—and there are lots of places I want to see yet—but under slightly different conditions of course. What do I mean—*slightly*!

I was in Paris some time ago and it was just like you've heard it is——well, maybe not quite, right now. Anyway, there is an Eiffel Tower and the Arc de Triomphe and such. And the people all speak French and drink wine—isn't that amazing? While I was there, I got hold of a fellow in our outfit (sounds like I got rough, doesn't it) who has been here before and professes to have a slight knowledge of perfume, whereupon we assaulted a little perfume shop which was quite, quite…anyway, impressive. By much sniffing and gesturing, a purchase was made. The gist of all this is that I sent some perfume to the women in my life, and if you don't get it, you're probably just as well off. I sent it to Mother and she can send it to you—if she gets it. If you see the same stuff in Woolworths for forty-nine cents, I will not be greatly surprised. One of the boys bought a little pin for seventy-five francs and as he was showing it to me, I noticed that it was made in Japan, and you can probably get it for a dime back home. Isn't the world a great place?

I am sure you are a good cook (you said you were), and I would certainly like to pull myself up to your festive board and make with the knife and fork. I imagine I will have to be *re-housebroken* before I do that. I lost my fork and knife some months ago and since then I have become very adept with a spoon—it's really quite an art. The bread-and-butter situation was at first quite difficult, but being an athletic sort of person, I soon conquered that. I have developed my right arm to such an extent that I could cut a piece of shoe leather with my spoon.

I have been trying for some time to get a letter to each and every one of my correspondents. You see how well I do. What I am getting at is that I'm going to sign off. Goodby, for now.

Love, Mac

PS Take it easy and don't chop any wood—it isn't good for a woman in your condition. I still say twins! Won't that be keen? You bet!

PS I'll have to send this to your old address as the return address on your letter was obliterated. Observe change in my address.

Package from Home December 7th 1944 France

Hello Beautiful!

A few short days ago I received a short crisp note written by your loving hands and photographed by the government's somewhat incapable ones. After much scrutiny, and no little amount of help from some tried-and-true mail reader friends of mine, I learned to my great surprise that I owe you a letter, and that, if nature can anywhere near be depended on, I, Mac Davis, will be an uncle by the time you have deciphered this composition.

Last night I received two packages, one from Uncle Dawson and Aunt Naomi. They were the first packages I have received since August (I put this in practically every letter I write —I don't know why). The packages from home contained such necessary commodities as soap, razor blades, etc. The soap I needed very badly, the razor blades not so much. After all, the government sells me two practically every week, new ones at that.

The package from Uncle Dawson and family contained a generous sample of all the delectable delicacies Aunt Naomi can bake. It was packed in a gallon can which is a very fine way to pack things. Dawson went one step better than everybody else and soldered the lid on and we (I have many helpful friends when occasions such as this arise) had one hell of a time getting the deal gutted. Besides very nearly slashing off a thumb or two, I broke the blade on some kid's puny little knife I was using. He voluntarily loaned it to me, so I wasn't responsible. I used to have a big all purpose knife. It was really a wicked looking thing I used to chop wood and butcher C-rations cans with, but I lost it—as per usual.

Duty calls, which is strictly a figure of speech. Anyway I'm going to quit pretty soon.

By the way I just finished reading *Turnabout* by Thorne Smith, and, in case you didn't know, it's not bad.

Since you are the mother of my first *niecphew*, I feel sure that you will overlook some important things concerning its health, such as orange juice and liver pills and one thing and another.

Leaving the care and training of this youth in your capable hands for the present, I remain your loving brother, Mac.

Return to Munich April 21, 1946

Dear Frances and Hayward,

Easter Sunday! I made it! I will give you a brief account of my trip and some of the strange happenings. Correction—there were no strange happenings. I boarded a derelict called The Sea Porpoise about April 7th. Of course, since I was aboard and in a hurry, the ship developed engine trouble 300 yards out of the port. But, they worked fast and in a mere twenty-four hours, we were on our merry way. It was a little crowded, there being 650 of us in a room or hold, which was sixty feet by sixty feet. This is impossible, but anyway, we did it. Bean soup with stew was the main course of our meal, and weak tea—the others. I did not become sick and I lost a little money playing the Yankee game of draw poker. Eight days to make Le Havre, where upon, we did debark (as the nautical term goes amongst sailors). The very unusual fact that I comprised a unit of men in myself now began to have its good and bad points. First, I had no one to tell me when and where to go for this and that, and I fell in with another group of soldiers and spent the night with them in what they call a "Tent City." The next morning, I and my 147 pounds of baggage hitch-hiked into Le Havre where I traded two US dollars for a handful of francs, bought a ticket on the train to Paris and was once again on my way. In Paris I caught another train through to Munich. This was quite a stroke of luck. All of the passengers were soldiers returning to Germany after spending furloughs in Paris. I just slipped in, as it were. Made good connections too. I was, all told, forty-five minutes in Paris.

Late the next night, April 18th, I arrived in Munich. Two hours later, I buzzed the buzzer of Biedersteiner apartment. The greetings were quite a thing, to say the least. Since then everything has been good and fine and I don't believe I have ever felt so contented.

Tuesday I will go to Frankfurt and report for duty, and then we will start to begin to make plans. I will write again when I know my new address. The address on this envelope is not mine. Another letter in three or four days. Love, Mac

Letter to Eldest Daughter about King-Hagan Post Speech

November 1968

Dear Sunta,

    Had a terribly traumatic week. Lost my glasses for one thing. My arms are just barely long enough for me to read without them. And I made a speech of four minutes in front of an audience of two hundred people! God, what suffering. What torture! The talking finally came off okay. But the getting ready almost killed me. Got drunk two times in one day—day before—trying to figure out what to say, or better yet, how to get out of it all. It was an American Legion folderol. Fiftieth thing since the end of World War I—and how I got hooked into that blast, I don't know. Native ignorance, I guess.

    "A Short History of the King-Hagan Post" was my assignment. A short thing to be read, I understood, when I reluctantly accepted this chore. To my dismay, I discovered no such paper existed, and I was expected not only to read it but also to compile it. That is—to write it. I was stunned to learn this.

    I thought about leaving home, abandoning my family, and going to Australia or Ethiopia or someplace—any place. So I went home and got drunk and sobered up, and reality grabbed me, and I realized I couldn't abandon my family.

    Then shame and egotism both grabbed me and I decided that I, by God, could talk for five minutes on any subject in the world and it was shameful to be so willy-nilly about it all. So I went down to the offices and attic of the American Legion and began to rummage through the records and junk. I took down notes, and when I finally got up to speak on that horrible night, my pockets bulged. I had enough notes to write a five-hundred page book. Not a very interesting book to be sure—but, boy, did I have notes! I was ready.

And then a terrible, mortifying thing happened. I did not know where in the program I would be called on, so every time the Master of Ceremonies got up, I got ready. I finally followed the principle speaker. An imported orator, who will someday be a candidate for the president of the United States, a man from whose mouth, words and phrases roll out like the sound from a phonograph record. Without a single note, without a podium to grasp and lean on, without a microphone, he scorned them all. He talked for thirty minutes. He bewitched the whole audience. He had the avid, concentrated attention of every soul in the house. I don't remember much of what he said, but I sure listened. He sat down to a thunderclap of applause.

He did all that without one single bit of humor. And that is what saved me. He sat down to all that applause and concentrated attention, and the MC called on me for a "short history of the post." I could hardly move. I could barely breathe. I was suddenly drenched in sweat. I finally stood up and stumbled to the podium and faced an absolutely silent audience with four hundred glazed eyes boring in on me, begging for an anticlimactic climax to all that blazing astounding rhetoric. And the same thought kept running through my mind. This is surely the most ludicrous, ridiculous, position that I have ever been in all my life. Nothing in childhood, Sunday school, war, or marriage ever reached this ridiculous point.

And so I stammered and stuttered awhile and told them it was not possible to follow an act like that. It broke them up and they laughed. They had been stone-cold serious for over an hour and they wanted to laugh. It wasn't all that funny, but they grabbed what I said and released themselves from all that soberness. And they saved my life.

So I skipped most of the notes from my five-hundred-page book and dredged out anything that could even remotely be called funny. Actually, I had, by this time, dropped most of my notes anyway.

I gave them about four sentences of history and about seven laughies and sat down to that bubbly sound—still sweating and weak. They sure didn't get much history.

A pretty stupid idea in the first place. A five-minute history of an idiot organization that's been raging for fifty years. If you ever get into a deal like that, you better look for the funny things, rare though they may be, because the most of it will sicken you with boredom.

Love, M.

Letter Commissioning Art by Michael Heffel, 1970

Drawing of Giacometti by Michael Heffel

Dear Mike,

You probably know that I am interested in the "Indian thing." Not in a scholastic way, cause I ain't built scholastically. And I am not much interested in the political hay-making thing of now, "Lo the poor Indian" and all that grunt. What I am interested in is a private interpretation of heroics.

And right now, I'm interested in the pictorial expression of it. I admire your pen drawing of Giacometti. I admire your pen work and I admire the doing of the man and the expression you have been influenced to make.

Enough of that, what I would like to have is a pen drawing of the Apache, Geronimo, and also one of the Modoc, Captain Jack. There are several photographs available of Geronimo. Of the Modoc, Captain Jack, I have seen only one.

To not draw it out further:

In the manner in which you have drawn Giacometti, I would like to have Captain Jack and Geronimo drawn.

I will give you $150.00 each to draw them on good material.

Enclosed my check for $100. Balance due when I see them.

Sincerely yours,
M. Davis.

Bad Day Letter to Kids in California, 1968

My day started on a zero note and has progressed throughout the day to even lower notes. I just weathered the last blow, which was to discover that the *Rowin & Martin's Laugh-In* has been canceled. So as to give Humphrey and Nixon a last half hour each to belabor a suffering public yet still some more with their fantastic abilities to talk continuously and incessantly, and yet never say anything. *Rowan & Martin's Laugh-In* is the one single show I watch, and I've been done a damn big injustice. I think I will vote for either Pat Paulsen or Red Hall. Probably be Paulsen because I wouldn't want to hurt Red Hall's feelings.

The first bad thing today was, of course, as always, the getting up and with it. But after two to three cups of coffee, my heart, as always, began again to beat, and I went forth to duties. Since the wheat is all planted and growing now, I am, for the first time in my life, on a self-arranging schedule of activities. It is all very fine, except in the mornings, I walk out the door and discover I have forgotten to arrange a schedule. This discombobulates me, and I usually go back into the house and have another cup of coffee and do some hasty scheduling.

Lately, however, I have not had this discombobulated feeling. I have my cattle assembled in two places and so the first order of business is to feed and check the cattle. This takes from one hour to all day. Today was an all-day cow-day, and nothing I did furthered my position as a successful stock man—unless you count bad experiences to have a generally broadening and enriching quality. Some people do, I know, but I have always looked upon this kind of enrichment with, what I believe they call, a baleful eye.

At any rate, if I still have your indulgence—the morning began by feeding these knot-headed, still-unhealthy calves I have here at home and checking my four expectant heifers. Sure enough, the knot heads still look like knot heads and one heifer is going to calve in a matter of hours or anytime. Got her into the barn—not always an easy task, but fairly simple this time.

Then down to the south pasture to check. They are grazing on alfalfa and sometimes this will kill them. Some cattle bloat on alfalfa. So I run down there every morning and evening to see if everybody is still healthy. This morning, everybody is healthy, but one six-week-old calf is gone. Very unusual, six-week-old calves don't ever get far from mama, she being the greenest pasture they will ever know. Search the pasture and other nearby pastures for two to three hours. No calf. Only good thought I had was that walking around in pastures on a clear, still day in early November is not unpleasant. Still no calf and that's bad.

Back home to see about the heifer. Bad. Hard birth. So out with the ropes and clamps and pulleys and on to midwifery. Granddad was with me by then. And we went at it with a will. Like we were birthing another Jesus Christ or something. And we didn't birth anything. We just finally heaved out a ninety-pound corpse. We groveled around in all that blood and slimy glup. I gave it artificial respiration, blew my breath down its nostrils, massaged its tongue, and finally beat its chest, and still it remained a corpse. It was so close to life, it breathed and blinked an eye when it was half out, but it never got its lungs full in time. A four-second life.

We washed and went to the house and Kay had a good beef stew and biscuits for us, and of course, coffee.

Then back to the south pasture to make another fruitless search and also inquiries at various dairies for a new-born calf to buy for any calf-less heifer. No success. I conclude the missing calf has been stolen.

Two gone in one day and then to be offered Nixon and Humphrey for *Rowan & Martin's*!

It's been a full day, but no scores. The full day is worth something, I suppose, but my eye is still baleful. I wonder if that's really the way to spell that word.

So what have you been doing? We'd like to hear. Your powers of description are not as meager as you believe. Tell all the Okies around there that it rained over the weekend and the wheat looks great.

Love, Dad

PS: A farmer from North Dakota came by yesterday in a big truck. He was peddling potatoes—of all things to peddle! He said that Dakota farmers live in hope and die in despair.

He was a Holdeman with the JC beard and all. And so doleful and sad, like he had just been unnailed from the cross himself.

I told him, "Hell, man, here in Oklahoma, we go through that hope and despair business nine times a day.

I bought a one hundred-pound bag of potatoes, and he left, still grim and sad. But still he had my five dollars!

Snow Day Letter February, 1971

Dear Ones,

You will find it hard to believe what is going on here. The snow is about two inches deep. The wind is big, about fifty miles per hour. We don't have any booze. The food supply is low. That is the children's opinion. I know we have enough food here for about ten years—counting the cattle, the hogs, and all that stuff. The horses and cats would keep everyone going for a month or more.

Jess and I managed to feed our cattle here. We kicked out the hay and told them to have at it.

We have $11,000 of cattle one mile west of here, on the Poetker 80. I hope I don't get brave enough to go try to take care of them.

After all, what is $11,000 worth of cattle when you have a son who is a multibillionaire I think he would loan me the money—if I should need it.

It is hard to believe this snow and wind.

We begin the game again.

Love, M.

Letter to Dad's cousin about his Dad

1970

After a long dry summer and fall, it rains. Yes, indeed…it rains and rains and rains. I think God misplaced the off button.

I have managed to get about seventy acres of wheat planted, but I have got about nine times that much yet to do. I am ready for dry weather.

One nice thing about a rainy day is that there is time to poke around at simple chores you have been putting off for three hundred years. I may clean out my clothes closet. On the other hand, I may not. Just the mystery of all the junk and things I will find in there has kept me from grubbing it all out for several years. You know—1948 checkbooks, a fine tweed suit bought in 1951, the absolutely last wool army shirt with stripes and moth holes. I have considered asking Kay to straighten it out, but on second thought, I don't want her to do that. I have some really good things back in that closet that nobody knows are good except me.

I don't believe I will get to the closet thing today. I had better wait for a twenty-day blizzard for that.

Thank you for reminding Dad about the physical checkup business. He is very obstinate about that and we don't talk about it. If he is not in good health, he is one of the world's greatest actors. He likes to work in the field. I have noticed that when we have the field operation done, our attitudes about the job are different. I am pleased and satisfied to have the thing done. He is a little down because there isn't more to do. He is an activist. He keeps a very precise routine in his daily life. Solid good breakfast at 6:30 at the Hi-Way Café. He will be showered, shaved, and suited up spic and span for the day before him. If it is field work, he will be wearing clean khakis. If it is business, he will be wearing a suit. If it is anything else, he will wear a sports shirt and slacks, and square-toed shoes. He usually has noon meal here at the farm. In the evening, he eats again in a restaurant. He seldom eats at home or alone. He knows everybody. Or everybody knows him. I don't know which is more accurate. He is frequently consulted by people of all ages for his views on land, money, and politics. It pleases him to give advice. It is usually short, brief, and once in a while, caustic. He knows that he knows what he is talking about. It is an admirable trait, although, I sometimes do not agree with him.

Mac.

Pony Purchase Letter

May 13, 1971

Glad you stopped by. Sorry I acted like a nervous wreck so much of the time. Kay says that it is because I am getting older, more sentimental, and all that. It was a surprising appraisal to me. I thought the business of sentiments and emotions worked the other way. Perhaps Kay is right. Anyway, I've said good-bye to you scores of times but the last one affected me most. I suppose Kay is right. Enough philosophy.

Yesterday, I sold some cattle, which is an all-day deal. Sorting, corralling, loading, hauling, waiting to see them sell, bidding to protect myself and property—all that.

In one ten-second period of irrationality and boredom, I put in four bids on two ponies, and, damn it, I bought them.

So now we have three horses. The least productive of all livestock a man can own.

One of them is a black and white, spotted, which Jess rides like a Comanche on the war path. In other words, it is a broken (trained) to-ride horse.

The other horse is the one that threw me off into some piles of rocks or posts, a something, that bruised me up quite a bit. This morning, I caught her and tied her to a tree in the yard.

My father came out early and his first question was "What's that tied to a tree?"

I told him it was a crazy pony that I intended to ride right after breakfast even if it killed me.

And he said, "No use to be killed by a horse."

To make a long story short, we put a bridle on the horse and then, while he held, I jumped astraddle the bareback horse. It is not a big horse and my legs dangled to the ground. Then we walked up and down the driveway about five times. Kay called it one of the more ludicrous sights she had witnessed. A seventy-five-year-old father leading a little black horse up and down the driveway with long-legged forty-eight–year-old son sitting on the black pony, grimly clutching the pony's mane. Enough.

Love, M.

Weekend at Roman Nose State Park

May, 1971

Dear Eldest,

The past two or three days have been far too complicated to get into. I mean, I wouldn't really know where to begin.

Actually, in reality, we took a short two-day trip down to Roman Nose Park where we all (family—two kids, mother, and father) stayed in a spic and span refrigerator-airconditioned, neat and clean cottage.

The children spent their time fishing, sixteen and a half minutes, no luck—paddle boating, eating, swimming, and, again, eating. Kay spent most of her time mothering and housekeeping. As is her wont, we took along enough things and supplies to sustain a two-year stay in the Gobi Desert.

Yours truly spent most of his time doing his usual thing. (For Christ sake! I'm beginning to write like Norman Mailer—he *used* to be good.) At any rate, I spent most of my waking time reading and drinking which are two of the things that most interest me. It is, as I said, at the beginning of the message, all too complicated to talk about.

I will give you three (maybe four) completely unassociated events that occurred. You have to understand that there were several hundred *unassociated* things.

1. At 4:30 a.m., I sat on the bank of a clear water stream and had some communication with Chief Roman Nose, long departed from this life. He was the last of the Cheyenne War chiefs—that is what the sign says at the entrance to Roman Nose Park. He gave his land back to the

government that usurped it (the land) in the first place, and, now, it is a great park.
2. That is hard to follow.
3. We made one wild-ass trip back home to feed the cattle and the cats and the dogs and sheep and also to water some neighbor's cattle that I had forgotten about. I mean, I forgot about telling him I would take care of them on Thursday.

I will never get to point five or six tonight. The main points I wanted to share with you are:
1. I am drinking Schweppes Soda water–which is almost as good as beer.
2. The June issue of Playboy magazine publishes an almost endless interview with Albert Speer. It is worth reading. The girl pictures in that issue are about the same as they were eleven years ago. In fact, they may be the same pictures. I don't know.

Love, M.

PS Number one: (This one is short.) Have you bought any land?

PS Number two: (Also short.) Why did you date your letter? Curious thing to do. For you, I mean.

PS Number three: Got a letter from Sylvia!

Vacationing at Red River
July 15, 1971

For the past four days, we have been shacked up in a rustic cabin on a creek called Red River, New Mexico. It has been quite restful for me. The rest of the crew has been knocking themselves out, riding horses and ski lifts and feeding hundreds of salmons eggs (a kind of trout bait) to the fish. Some miracle happened yesterday, and they caught enough little trouts to almost cover the bottom of a skillet, so we had fish for dinner. Tomorrow, we head back to Oklahoma. We could make it in about a heavy ten-hour run, but I expect we will drag it out. It is surprising how we got so high up in the mountains without it bothering me much. I outwitted myself and so the trip was rather tensionless for me. I drove the flat-land country of the OK panhandle, and when the first mountain peak loomed in the distance, I said to Kay, "Okay, Baby, you take it from here." And then I set forth to reading the three months of magazines I'm behind. Never raised my head until we got here. Oh well, not really. It was a nice trip.

Our cabin, as they call it, sets about fourteen feet from the banks of the stream and about forty feet from a kind of log bridge that divides the Lewis Ranch resort. I sit on the porch and read, watch the stream, observe the people strolling by, consent sometimes to casual conversation with the passersby, who if you just nod at them, they usually break out with something like, "I'm from Dallas. Where are you from?" A couple of times, I've been tempted to say "I'm from Hong Kong," but I never have. It is a kind of gentle place, and I wouldn't want to startle anyone. Most of the people around are young married couples with two or three little kids or they are older couples with expensive travel rigs and brand new clothes, flashy fishing rigs, trying to squeeze some little bit more of adventure from their lives. It is the easiest place to start a conversation, and it also affords the easiest way to stop one. To stop one (conversation) you just say, "I'm cooking some beans, it's been nice to meet you. I'll see you later, I have to go stir the beans. Wife and kids are out riding horses." Everybody knows beans have to be stirred. So they move right on down to the fishing place or creek or store or whatever.

There is a lot more to tell, but I think I will go read some more.

Love, M.

PS: [The wayward young relative] finally, after two weeks and one day, confessed to his mother that he did take the money. I'm glad to have that part of it over, but what to do now to get it all straightened out is the problem. Granddad lost eleven pounds in the last two weeks worrying about it and sweating him out.

Take care. It was good to see you.

Love, M.

Birthday Letter to Sunta in Tokyo, Japan, 1989

Mac and eldest daughter, Sunta

It has been a long time since I have written to you. I think about you every day, and, in my mind, I always wish you good health and a serene day, but it would be tiresome for you if I wrote that down on a notepad and sent it to you every day. Wouldn't it?

I read the short stories by Orwell which you sent. That was a very nice present. Imagine my daughter tearing up a book just to send me a good story.

It may surprise you that the coal mine story set my mind off into the byways of memory in ways that surprised me. I thought of people and little remarks that had not crossed my mind in decades.

In the army, in England, just before the invasion, I was in a company with three lads from West Virginia. Coal miners, sons and nephews of coal miners, and although they were young, like we all were, early twenties, they had worked several years in the mines. Their physical development was similar to what Orwell describes. In fact, one was an exaggeration of what Orwell described being about three feet wide across the shoulders and a foot wide across the butt. They were hard as a rock and tough as a boot. The physical requirements of soldiering were a relaxing interlude in their lives.

But the thing I remember most about them was their calmness and a kind of gentleness coupled with a flinty-eyed hardness. They looked the world straight in the face and made up their minds pretty quick. Friend or foe, take your pick.

We were split into detachments before we went into France, and I never saw but one of them again. I was on MP duty for our regiment one night in a French town. Troisfontaines, I think. We were making our way, my partner and I, down a narrow street, putting in time, waiting for relief when up ahead of us three GIs kind of erupted out of a joint. They were talking loud, feeling good and about half drunk. One of them was the wide-and-narrow coal miner. We were all standing there in the street joking and so forth when I saw three other GIs approaching. They weren't talking or laughing, just ambling along. They were black boys from a truck company that hauled gasoline and ammo to the front. They didn't get to come to town often. We were still segregated then. To me they were more foreign than the French.

We stood there watching them approach. Suddenly, the coal miner let out a great shout and ran toward them. "George, George," he was shouting. "George! What are you doing here?" They embraced like a father and son, and the coal miner lifted the black guy off the ground and swung him around in a circle just beside himself with joy and exuberance. It was to me an absolutely astonishing scene.

They stood for a minute or two there in the street and laughed and slapped each other on the back. Then the black guy went over to his buddies, and the coal miner came back to us. "That was George," he said. "George, from West Virginia. We were boys together."

I suppose I could write a lot of stuff about why that isolated little happening stays so vividly in my memory, but it wouldn't have anything to do with coal miners.

Reading about coal miners reminded me that when my grandpa and grandma Davis came to this country, this place where I live, one of the reasons for coming here was to escape the coal mines of Missouri. I bet you didn't know that.

I remember the story like this: My great grandpa Davis owned a farm near Lexington, Missouri. He was also a Methodist preacher and a veteran of the Civil War. He had also been a prisoner of war for several months where he survived on a short ration of corn meal and an occasional rat. Being a religious man, he believed that God meted out rewards and punishments according to man's daily activity, and he told his children and his grandchildren, and they told me, that he believed he became a prisoner of war on account of his sinful activities the day before he was captured. On the day before he was captured, his outfit was trekking through the countryside, and he was suffering great hunger. In a moment of what he considered weakness, he allowed himself to raid a farmer's smokehouse where he snatched down a smoked ham to relieve his hunger. He stole the ham and the Lord arranged to have him captured next day and thrown into a miserable POW camp. On the farm near Lexington, there was a seam of coal which my great grandfather leased to a coal company with the stipulation that his sons would be given jobs as miners to mine the coal.

My grandma was young then and already headstrong, so she said, "We will go to Oklahoma where the land is new and cheap and it is more healthful to be a farmer in the open air than to be a miner underneath the earth." I don't know if that is exactly what she said, but it was something like that, and I have always thought it was a wise thing for her to have said and done. And when her husband died at the age of thirty-one and left her with three small sons, she was smart enough not to go back to Missouri and the coal mines but stayed right here in Oklahoma, where God knows, there is certainly plenty of air—even though it may not be as fresh as it was ninety-five years ago.

One other thing that really impressed me about coal mining was my great uncle George's coughing fit one snowy morn back in the 1930s. (This tale has two Georges in it but that is just coincidental). My great-uncle George was my grandpa's brother, and he stayed in Missouri for several years where he worked in the mines. He and his wife finally had enough of coal and moved to South Texas (south is capitalized in this case) where he operated a dairy until his retirement. He was only forty miles from the Gulf of Mexico so he too got to live a good part of his life in the fresh air—not enough, but what he carried with him, forever a reminder of his life in the mines.

It was a snowy morning and Uncle George and I were standing in the yard watching the snow fall when he began to hack and cough. Finally, he spat out a great gob of black goop and besmirched the snow.

"What in the world is that Uncle George?"

"Coal dust, son," he said. "Forty-year-old coal dust."

Now is March 27, several days later, and I guess I am through with Mr. Orwell and his coal mine story. In fact, I was writing this line about an hour ago when Kay called me to supper. I forgot to punch the right button and now that I am back on the machine. I see that I have lost all that I had written before. Well, anyway, I have been reading a lot of what can only be called "light stuff." Three novels by William Douglas, a retired military guy, who writes historical novels about Oklahoma. He filched a little quirky stuff from *True Grit* and *Butch Cassidy and the Sundance*

Kid, but I guess that's all right. Then I have read three Indian tales written by some doctor up in some Kansas town. He casts his stories in an earlier time than any I have read—the Plains Indians in the sixteenth century—when they first stole horses from the conquistadors. Kind of romantic fairytales, really. Good stories for young boys who are interested in anthropology.

And Jess gave me a book, *Shanghai Tango*, a kind of Indiana Jones tale about life in China, circa 1931, with just enough political stuff about Chinese warlords, Japanese spies, British colonials, and so forth to hang it together. One of the main characters, of which there are several, is a stranded showgirl from New Jersey who travels with a trained ape, an old trained ape with whom she dances the tango for all who care to pay. In thinking back, I believe the ape was the most believable character in the story—but it was fun. And then I found a book in a box of Kay's bargains entitled *Far Eastern War 1937-1941* by a guy named Quigley. It was published in 1941 and is a kind of intelligence report on China and Japan. Man! I have just gotten started on it and I didn't know all that stuff. They spent a long time getting ready for the big war—I mean old WWII, and they were ready. And—but I will have to read more.

Kay took the plunge and enrolled in the OU degree program. Right now, she is struggling with her first paper. She and her friend go down to a Norman for their first five-day seminar. Isn't that something? No telling what she will do—could be anything.

Now it is March 29. Your birthday. Happy Birthday. Born in the Schwabinger Krankenhaus. How many years ago? Not many. What a wonderment. Someday, I will tell you about it because I am sure you don't remember much about it.

A week or so ago, I went out to Colorado with JB to look at the country and the wheat and so forth. The wheat looked good. Real good. Maybe this is the big year. Anyway, I also arranged to sell a quarter of land for a fair price and that will relieve some of the money pressure on me which, of course, makes the future look bloomier. I didn't raise as many dollars as I wanted to, but then I didn't sell as much as I was planning to. The wheat here also looks very good. But there are always buts in this business. We had a freezing condition last week, which may have damaged the tiny, tiny heads just now forming in the plant. I remember a few years ago when you were here on your birthday and we had a light freeze which did damage the wheat some. Empty heads at harvest time. Not a lot, but some.

Everyone in the immediate family seems to be healthy. Frances is still home but is working part time at home. Land title work. She must be good at that business. Her boss sends out piles of documents and papers and she analyzes the legalities of it all. It is a mystery to most people, property titles, I mean. Same thing with automobiles. Every kid in high school ought to go through a short course on property titles and the mechanics of automobiles. It would clear up a lot of frustrating mysteries for people. And insurance companies, too. If we knew more about how insurance companies work, I am sure we would soon figure out how to do without them. I think they have a hammer-lock on society. I am prejudiced.

Time to wind this up. I hope you enjoyed your vacation and are happy with the school and your house and everything. Take care. Love, Papa

Broke Down in Hillsboro TX Letter

November 16, 1982, Tuesday
Hillsboro, Texas, Travel Trailer
185 yards West of Interstate 35

Dear Sunta and Augie,

Travel is broadening, and here we are being broadened in Hillsboro, Texas. Meanwhile, our bank account is being narrowed and some mechanics at the local Ford garage are making what I hope is an honest living rebuilding the motor of our pickup truck. We have been without wheels (not counting the ones on this travel coach) since Friday night 10:45 p.m. when the crank shaft broke while we were tooling down on the interstate on our way to Padre Island, Texas. Yesterday, the head honcho at the garage told us the thing might possibly be ready sometime on Wednesday if all the parts come from Dallas etc., etc.

It is not exactly exciting here in this makeshift park, but it is not really bad. There is plenty of leisure time for reading and taking care of house keeping chores. It is surprising how many little things there are to do such as emptying the waste tanks and replenishing the water tank and wondering why the water pump makes so much noise and why it is impossible to light the furnace. All in all, we are very comfortable and our personal relationship is close.

Up until a couple of hours ago, our neighbors offered quite a bit of diversion. They are (were) an elderly couple, traveling also to South Texas for the winter, who met with misfortune on the interstate. They (she) jackknifed their rig and had to be towed in. The damage to their car and trailer was not real serious, but getting it all back together kept the old man happily engaged for the best part of their days. I even helped a little—mostly by handing him tools and making frequent trips to see if the left turn signal or the brake light or the stop light or if anything else might finally be working. It is amazing how many different ways six wires can be put together before the right combination turns up—kind of a Rubik's Cube thing.

Have been reading George Gilder's book, *Wealth and Poverty*, which you will find very interesting, I am sure. Will send you a copy as soon as we move on to more urban areas. Now, it is time for my morning nap, and I will stop scribbling. Thanks you for recent cards and letters. Wish you success at the fairs.

Love, Mac

PS: When I quit writing, I didn't know I had all this blank space left (as we are running short on writing paper, I was only allotted two sheets for this letter) The book *Wealth and Poverty* is a treatise on capitalism and the economic situation today. That sounds like dry going, but is not. It is more a treatise on morality, I think. The writer is very kind and thoughtful, I think, and even footnotes the title to one chapter called "The Supply Side (Economics)" with * "This is a chapter on the theory of supply-side economics and may be safely passed over by readers who prefer a less abstract exposition of the subject." Wasn't that thoughtful? I read it anyway, and I am glad I did. Kay is still fumbling through the Dallas Sunday paper.

Now, I will quit!

Summer Farming

Saturday, July 31, 1971

The summer goes on. What else can it do? We have enjoyed very pleasant weather the past two to three days while we wait for things to dry out so we can "get back to the fields." In other words, we had some rain. I thought last Tuesday would never end as I bucketed back and forth across the big field up north, rough ground. It was hot and rough and, of course, dusty. The old mind went dull, and several times, I found myself asking myself, "If you are so goddamn smart, Davis, what are you doing here?" or with great pity, I would acknowledge to myself, "Getting a little old and stiff for this drill." Finally, the day ended and the rains came that night, started at 12:36 a.m. Wednesday, in fact—and the next morning, I felt just really grand. And Wednesday night, it rained again and so we are waiting for it to dry out! But Monday and Tuesday, man! We jerked the machines over 340 acres in two days.

Yesterday and today have been home-rec days. It's been honey-do and dad-come-here time.

Tanya has suddenly developed a missionary zeal to train a black pony I bought some months ago (The SOB threw me onto the hard ground the day after I gave it a good home) and Jess is bound to make a real hill scrambler out of his weak-lunged three horsepower minibike. It has a kind of lawnmower type of engine, which is the strongest part of its many weaknesses. The thing starts with one of those rope-wind-pray-lunge deals—same as an ordinary damn lawnmower. Jess is strong enough to pull the rope thing, but he simply is not long enough. The rope is longer than his arm, in other words.

So between his cries for help and Tanya's pleas for counsel on horse sense and my own frustrations with the freaky lawn mower, it has been an active period of family-at-home life.

Yesterday afternoon, by some quirk of events (diplomatic skill—I sent one of them north with the horse and one of them south with the bike and I shut off the lawn mower), I came into the house, popped a can of beer, flopped into a chair and told Kay (who was doing something at the stove) that the only salvation for mankind rests on the proposition that all gasoline engines and horses be buried at sea somewhere in the Antarctic oceans. I was ready to embrace the Stone Age culture.

I know that horses are animals and that the training of them involves a kind of psychological approach coupled with some brutish physical leverage, which all takes time and experience to understand and apply.

What I don't understand is why or how nobody has developed a simple gasoline engine. They are rolling around on the moon today with some kind of cart that costs 1.5 million dollars per mile to operate. They are going to drive the thing twenty-two miles and abandon it. Glory! Hallelujah!

I wish somebody would invent a simple lawnmower engine, so we could put it on the bike. A brace of goats and a sharp machete will do for the lawn. To hell with the mower.

Love, M.

PS: And a special curse on gasoline engines.

PS: Give credit due when credit is due—when they work, they work.

PS: We are going to get a Honda 90 I think.

PS: Man heaps curses upon himself.

"Ta-ta!" the English say. Strange people, the English. You will forgive me, bless me that I don't go into that.

Love, M.

Later: I have read another quotation from *The Devil's Dictionary*. It was written by Ambrose Bierce, and, someday, I would like to see (have) an actual copy of this strange (maybe mythical) book.

> *Mind: A mysterious form of matter secreted by the brain. Its chief activity consists in the endeavor to ascertain its own nature, the futility of the attempt being due to the fact that it has nothing but itself to know itself with.*

I have read quotations from this book a hundred times but I have never seen it. Your newspapers and magazines, I have read with great interest. In fact, I gave a copy of *Mother Earth News* to Skip who seemed intrigued. He flashed up here July 20th in his new VW. He is still the same somber character—now he has a mustache, a bushy one—and he was preparing himself for a trip East (DC) to see his "daddy," he said, with one eye closed. He was skeptical—large money was hinted at—but I know those goddamned people. The East Coast moneyed families, and so does he. You actually get (inherit) the big family funds fourteen seconds before they nail the lid onto your coffin. The old New England bankers and other pirates really knew how to hang onto the dough. I am going to rest awhile. Bye-bye.

Love, M.

Practical Joke on Bill McCue

Letter to Kids

Mar 1, 1972

So we had two of the hottest days ever known for February 28 and February 29 in Oklahoma history, and today, it is so miserably cold and windy that even the cattle won't leave their shelter.

Not much to write about. I'm personally (bad style) getting tired of news. In the last two days, three people I knew died, another one discovered he had lung cancer, and a fifth one crashed a motorcycle.

Time to hear a funny story.

Have you ever been involved in a practical joke? They used to be quite common. Haven't even heard about one for years. People used to go to great lengths to pull off a good one. A form of diversion in a less frenetic time. Read some of H. Allen Smith's *The Practical Joker* or maybe it is called *The Complete Practical Joker*.

The greatest ones are the ones that drag out the longest. I've been mulling over one for about thirty-five years. One of these days, I'm just going to do a Dick Tracy thing and find out about it. But that's another story.

I was going to tell you about some extraordinary practical jokes I have heard about but how can I let that last thing just drop?

Do you know about stallions and how they are publicized and advertised? By handbills and newspaper announcements. You know that stallions have strange names. In fact, all registered animals have strange and often flamboyant names.

You have heard of Man o' War, Native Dancer—the great race horses. There is the great Domino line in Hereford cattle. There must be not less than 10,000 Hereford cattle with an official name of Domino (i.e. Jack Domino Vll, Mary Ann Domino ll etc.). Quarter horses are often given very common names such as John Smith, Henry Jackson etc.

Once when I was a kid, there appeared an overly large AD in the local paper:

STANDING AT STUD

in

ARAPAHO OKLA

BILL MCCUE

Fee $20.00

Guaranteed

The Throw to Stand and Nurse

By Appointment

Now, was there really a stallion named Bill McCue in Arapaho in 1935? Or was that just some local wag's idea of a joke on my grandpa?

I think it was a joke, and, boy, would I like to have a copy of that paper.

Love, M.

Stepped On

Letter to Sunta in California

June 11, 1971

It is 6:30 AM. Raining like it did in Noah's day. We are in the middle of a poor harvest, and now, it rains and rains and rains. I keep telling myself to take the long view. All this beautiful rain will make next year's crop a big one.

Which brings to mind two old sayings: "Farmers work for next year's prosperity," and "Farmers live in hope and die in despair." Both of these sayings are utter nonsense.

Farmers live just like anyone else—live the life, enjoy the life, but keep an eye out for the pitfalls, bear traps, wild Indians, and mad politicians.

So I will tell you something astonishing, pitiful, and at the same time, rather funny.

My cousin Cal has a bull with what we decided yesterday was some disorder with his penis. Which, of course, is a serious matter if you have cows and hope for them to raise calves.

So we loaded him up into my old pickup and took him to the veterinarian. This was no simple task since he was in a pasture seven miles west of here out in the hills. We located him three quarters of a mile from the loading corral in the far corner of the pasture. He was reluctant to our idea. With God's help and our brilliant wit, we eventually got him loaded.

We hauled him to town to the veterinarians' clinic. The place was closed up. Vacation time for the veterinarians.

We went to my cousin's place and refreshed ourselves with several quarts of iced tea and some sandwiches.

Then we telephoned a veterinarian in Okeene, and he told us to come on down to his house. We lurched the twenty miles down to Okeene.

The bull, you understand, was getting restless. He kept banging around in the rack and his shifting weight made steering the old pickup more difficult than usual.

We got to Okeene and DVM Sylvan Hayworth came out to examine the bull. The bull's penis was hanging four or five inches out of his sheath—which is not natural. It was also swollen to about three times its normal size. Cal and I had concluded he had some kind of infection or disease.

The DVM studied the situation for a minute or so. "There is no disease and there is no infection. It is just bruised. He stepped on it."

I said, "What did you say?"

"It is an undesirable characteristic of Angus bulls to let it all hang out after they service a cow. They have short legs. The penis drags on the ground and the idiots frequently step on it and since they weigh about 1200 pounds, that tends to bruise the penis," said the august DVM.

"It is also," he continued, "the reason why I don't keep Angus bulls on my ranch."

After we had absorbed this astounding information, we asked him what was to be done.

So he told us there is nothing medically to be done and advised us to pen him away from the herd, and wait one week for nature to correct the condition. If nature didn't correct things, take him to market and sell him for hamburgers.

The man was not without humor. "Sometimes, it will heal with a crook in it and this causes embarrassing situations in mixed company."

He wanted no fee for this consultation and invited us into his garage to examine a renovated 1926 Model T Ford roadster. It was a marvelous machine and he took us each for a drive in it.

On the way home, we bought a six-pack of Coors and discussed the oddities of things in general.

The bull, weary of the business, simply laid down and rested. Other than that, yesterday afternoon was uneventful. How did your day go?

Love, M.

Letter to Jess and Calleen from Palenque, Mexico

November 20, 1988

Dear Jess and Calleen,

So far...so good. After we got the clutch linkage fixed up in McAllen, Texas, Tuesday (November 15) morning and after Kay shopped for just a few more things, we plunged into Mexico.

Coming out of the passport vehicle registration barn and passing the inspector of papers and his interpreter (loose use of the word); twelve bucks, and ten for the inspector, and two for the grunter, we narrowly missed a truck and our first turn.

In two minutes, we were confused, but after bumping along for a mile or so, we got lined out and on our way down squalor lane. Ten miles into Mexico, the customs officer flagged us down. One guy sternly said, after it was definitely established that we spoke no Spanish, pointing to the back, "Open up." I think I heard him groan a bit when the door swung open. He asked me questions I couldn't understand and I gave him answers he couldn't understand. He pointed two or three times, and finally, I started to climb in and haul the stuff out. He tapped me on the shoulder and said, "No, no. Okay, okay. Go." I slammed the door shut, handed him six or seven dollars and said *gracias* or something like that, whereupon he cheerfully and clearly said, "Good for you." And that's all there was to it.

Eggs, Immigrants, and Doctors Letter

September 24, 1996

While I am impatiently waiting for two eggs to boil, I will write to you. Yesterday, we got the book package with newspaper. I read the immigration article. Good. I have noticed that situation for some time. Mexicans, Vietnamese, work hard and move along. There are three or four Mexican families in the community, and they do well. Across the street from Fran's house lives a Vietnamese couple that remind me of two bees. One was out sweeping the street gutter last time I saw them! Spic and span—one car, one pickup on the driveway sparkling like a showroom display.

One hour later. So I ate the egg and moved the tractor to the Poetker 80 and the rain began to fall! We are having a wet fall which is just as frustrating as a dry spring.

At 11 a.m., I have a doctor's appointment with a new wizard who is going to investigate my sleep patterns. Which I thought were perfectly fine but Kay told Dr. Z they seemed weird to her. Kay says I breathe deeply (when I am asleep) for nine breaths, then I stop breathing for thirteen seconds. One sleepless night, she passed the time doing this timing check. One time! Now I'm being examined by a sleep wizard.

This reminds me of an interesting article in *Harpers*—June issue, I believe—which talks about the pharmaceutical companies and all the wonderful drugs they are pushing onto the mentally stressed; a classification that applies to 99.6 percent of the population according to the psycho-babble folks. It seems to me there is a great plot or plan to switch us all from the beneficial effects of tobacco, coffee, booze, and pot to Prozac, Valium, and seven hundred other expensive drugs. Anyway, it is interesting. The very best part is the cover illustration for the article: "Oh How Happy We Will Be." I am thinking about framing it and hanging it on the bathroom mirror. It would be kind of an upbeat kick-start for the day while I scrub my false teeth and trim my mustache.

Next day, 10 a.m. So yesterday's rainy morning was just a drizzle and I harrowed down the Poetker 80 in the afternoon and Jess started planting about 7:30 p.m. (he has powerful lights over the whole rig) and drilled for two hours. During the night, it rained 1.8 inches! Today, it is too wet to do anything outside—and the annual threshing be starts tomorrow!

Kay finished baking over 500 rolls—small rolls—for the butter making demonstration tomorrow at the threshing bee. They—not me—are going to milk the cow, separate the cream, churn the butter, dab it on the roll, and hand it out to any of the 847 sixth-grade kids who are scheduled to visit the threshing bee tomorrow, who might want to taste real butter on a real piece of bread, after watching the cow being milked and all the rest of it, some of those kids will probably never eat butter—ever.

Now, I am going to town to mail this letter, drink a cup of coffee with the loafers at the Co-op, buy a newspaper, and come home to wait for dry weather.

Love you and miss you. Take care.
Papa

Letter of Response for Offer to Buy Pickup

February 6, 1996
Miss Beth Boyd
Okemah, Okla., 74859

Dear Miss Boyd,

Please pardon me for waiting so long to answer your letter of inquiry about the old pickup.

Unfortunately for you (or maybe it is fortunate), the pickup is not available. Shortly after the story appeared in the magazine, a lady drove into my yard, not a young lady, "That's my dad's old pickup," she said. "The day he drove it home, brand new, he was as proud as the King of Siam."

So you can guess what happened. She wants the pickup. Her husband wasn't very excited about it, but she was sure her son and grandson would be excited.

Thank you for writing to me. I like the tone of your letter and I would bet that you are going to get along just fine in this life. One little disappointment won't slow you down much.

Good luck in the hog business or whatever you turn to.

Sincerely yours,
McWilliam Davis

Last Notes and e-mails

Letter to Morris' Niece re Memorial Day June 2, 1997

On Memorial Day, my wife, Kay, and I went to the cemetery to decorate the family's graves and to attend the small ceremony that the American Legion conducts every year in memory of all veterans of the various wars. Part of the preparation for this memorial service is the marking of each veteran's grave with a small American flag. I find it quite impressive.

The stones that you have had set for Morris and Verna's graves are quite nice and we appreciate you having had Mr. Chuck Obermiller take care of that. The cemetery is always well cared for by the city. I appreciate that, and I am sure you do too.

With your approval, I would like to have Mr. Obermiller arrange to have a military marker set at Morris's grave site. This is a bronze, plate-type marker set flat at ground level at the foot of the grave. It is about twenty-four by eighteen inches and simply states name, rank, organization, and dates of service. I will be happy to take care of the details if you approve. The cost is small, and we will take care of that. We will need a copy of his military discharge which you can send to either Mr. Obermiller or to me. I might further tell you that the marker is a standard government issued marker. It will not show any information such as serial number, religious statements, or affiliation with any veteran's organizations. If you have any questions or want more information, I am happy to oblige you.

Sincerely yours,
McWilliam Davis

E-mail to kids in Nagasaki March 27 1997

Dear Sunta and Augie,

First, congratulations on selling a lamp. Maybe you will become the leading *gaijin* Japanese lamp-maker in all of Japan. I hope so. Yesterday, Kay and I went down to the city to visit my doctors—the knife man and mad cardiologist—who prescribe medicines and makes jokes. I look just lovely they said. Nice heart, nice lungs, nice scabs, nice color. Everybody always talks about nice color. Even just an ordinary praying friend feels qualified to comment on an invalid's nice color.

Well, I walked for twenty minutes—steady. Pretty stiff south breeze. I am SOB, which stands for "somewhat out of breath" on walking chart. We keep this chart up to date. How far did I walk, how long, etc., and nobody has given me a grade yet! I am getting kind of discouraged. Maybe I'll just mail it to Zielinski.

Love, Mac

Will keep trying to send this. If it "times out," I'll just keep trying. Maybe you'll get five of this same letter or maybe none. We'll see. Happy Birthday.

E-mail to kids in Nagaski April 3, 1997

Will do a few lines (Mac). Fingers still not very dexterous—maybe they never were. Am getting along okay, I think. Getting up and suiting up for the day seems to be a pretty big deal. I am thinking about compiling a check list so I don't forget anything or repeat anything. I usually forget to shave until I am all gussied up for my morning walk. I walk about half a mile in ten or eleven minutes. Am reading more everyday. My interest span seems to have shortened. I finally finished that "Garlic whatever" about Lo Pan. It was not very good from my point of view. Repetitious violence and barbarity among the peasants and the government guards. I don't know how they all tolerate so much inhumanity from each other. Maybe it is changing now in China.

My handling of the demon nicotine has not been perfect. Yesterday, I smoked three cigs. plus lighting up two or three snipes (butts) Kay left in the garage smoking lounge—secretly, of course, I do this stuff. It seems like two or three puffs is all I really want. What I want is just to feel a tad more up. I guess everybody wants that, *nicht wahr?* Well, I am just about ready for another one of the big activities of the morning. I am going to town to buy the morning paper!

The big news, of course, is the Timothy McVeigh trial, which started Monday. Everybody is going to be offered more details and more *thoughtful* analysis than they want. So now, I close. I pray you have a fine day. The main thing is to enjoy the day. I love you both and I am proud of you. Ta-ta.

Last e-mail from the farm

May 21, 1997

Good morning Sunta and Augie,

Just got back from morning walk. Still morning, lots of bugs clouded around, went with us. They flew, we walked. Was nice to talk with you on the phone. Received your birthday message to Calleen. Nik just called from the Shadetree. She's saving me the remaining three sweet basil plants they have. None of the basil seed I planted came up. Old seed. What is up in the garden looks great considering the three-day-late freeze awhile back and two gully washers after that. Can't wait for your news ten days from now. The poppy plant (that stayed green all winter in the flower box by the kitchen window) is being phenomenal. Up to yesterday, one bloom opened each morning about seven. When I get up, the bud is showing some color, pushing off the pod from around it. By about seven thirty, the pod is lying somewhere fairly far away and the flower is free to open and does—fast. The blooms really only last about two days. We had a rain and cloudy skies day before yesterday, and today, ten flowers opened. I took a picture of yesterday of Mac sitting by them. Will send. Calleen says the poppies we saw in Santa Fe were much bigger. They were in a plaza, protected on all sides, and probably babied a lot. Maybe next year, I will baby these. Fun to watch. End of school finally here. All activities over. Jess and Calleen made their annual trek to the national motocross races in Ft. Worth with children. Stayed at Ed and Sue's. Bought their old car for Nikki, and Jess is fixing it up. She will be able to get her license in one year. Periodically, Nikki disappears. That mystery was finally solved when they found her sitting in the car. Now, when Nikki can't be found, they just go up to the car and there she is—just sitting there in it. Going to be a long year for her. Kay

Mac here. We hoofed about a mile today. A nice stroll. Kay wants to walk fast, but I don't. I amble. An ambler can go further than a fast strider. The hare and the tortoise thing, you know. I feel pretty good most of the time, I just can't do much of anything that exerts me. I guess I will get used to it—either that, or get stronger. Several people have told me that it takes about a year to gain some of your strength back. It looks to me like by the time one gets one's strength back, one could be—at the same time, getting weaker because of advancing old age. A hell of a note. I sit around thinking of all the neat things I could be doing like writing letters or getting my junk in better order, but then I get bogged down on where to start. Then I go to an AA meeting and lecture the troubled souls on the necessity of getting busy. Do something, I say, don't just sit around planning to do something. Get after it. It exhausts me, and I myself do nothing. I have been thinking about my first business venture and all the lifelong lessons I learned from it. I may write a marble story. Someday. The kid that taught me these lessons had coal black hair, a pale freckled face, and bright blue eyes. What a shyster. A dead-shot hustler. He bankrupted me. Won every last marble I owned. I wonder what happened to him. I bet he is a rich man.

Now I am going to quit and look for papers to send you. Enjoy the day.

Love, love, love,
Papa

Munich and World War II Memories

Munich

Occupation of Munich

We occupied Munich the third of May, if I remember correctly. The war ended on the eigth of May. And what began on the Normandy beach twenty-five years ago, tomorrow, was done. The war machine shut down to cool its motor.

I was with a small detachment occupying the town hall. Our mission was to govern the city. There were fewer than thirty of us. The population of Munich was over one million and may even be two million. I don't know. I suppose I could look it up but what's the difference.

We had fantastic authority. Every one of us—I was a corporal at the time exercising the power of a colonel.

As pasha of the transportation department, dispatcher, and proprietor I could dispense uncommon merchandise. Wheels to almost anywhere.

I ruled this enviable domain with a partner, Johnny Cerro, a gregarious Italian chap from Beverly, Mass. who approached everything in daily life with the high-flung passion of teenage love and the inborn wisdom of fifty generations of Sicilian peasants. He was the old man of our fiefdom, being, at that time, about twenty-three or twenty-four years of age. I recall the splendor of that unbelievably wonderful summer from time to time and realize that Johnny was the blood and muscle of our operation, and that I was the nerves and brains of it.

After all, it was I who developed the trip-ticket thing that kept track of our vehicles of which we had a multitude.

In addition to our generous supply of strictly GI vehicles, reconnaissance cars and all that, we had enlarged our motor-pool and jazzed it up. I might say, too, by exercising our rights and power and imagination.

We had, for instance, one afternoon discovered, liberated, and commandeered an entire taxicab company, complete with drivers. During that same week, we also found, liberated, commandeered, and hauled into our lot some ten or twelve really beautiful Mercedes-Benz. One particular plum I remember was a big black convertible sedan with three rows of seats. These cars were just extras, so to speak, dispensed, dispatched, released, and used at our whim and/or pleasure.

Such was my position in early June, when a pale looking second lieutenant presented himself to my dispatcher's window in the courtyard of the Munich Rathaus. His emaciated appearance was not unusual. We, our detachment, had eighty or ninety thousand concentration camp people that we were theoretically caring for. Delousing them with pump gins full of medicinal powders seemed to be the big move at the time.

I digress, I know. I remember our medic sergeant, our only one, now that I think about it, coming into our billet one night. He was dead tired and haggard beyond belief. I asked him to come to a party—liberated Russian slave girls and nine million gallons of wine. He declined, "I've sprayed and dusted not less than 5,000 armpits and crotches today and you are the last human I want to see today. Good night".

Well, such was the time and so Lieutenant Brownfelder's emaciated appearance was not, in itself, strange. His eyes were memorable. They begged sympathy and yet they defied sentiment. He was his own man. The papers he handed in through the window were the most inclusively authoritative military orders I have ever read. I can't remember positively, but it hung in my mind that they were signed by General Eisenhower. At any rate, the gist of the paper directed that everyone and anyone in the Allied Command help this man, the bearer of these order, to the lengths of his authority.

He wanted a car, transportation, wheels. How simple for me.

I gave him the best chauffeured Mercedes we had. He checked it in that evening with three hundred kilometers on the meter. He turned up first one in line the next morning, and I gave him the same car and, of course, the same driver. The drivers actually owned their cars and the taxi company deal was some kind of cooperative thing. I can't recall that man's name. His first name was Hans, I remember that. The number of his hack was 2220. He would say that when he came to the window.

After a while, I learned that Lt. Brownfelder had been shot down over the city of Munich some year or so before and was taken prisoner by the Germans. He had been treated, he said, all in all, fairly. They gave him to eat what they ate. Potatoes. He had

had them boiled, baked, raw, fried, and all the other 435,000 ways potatoes can be served. Potatoes are to Europe what rice is to the Asians and to what the meat of bears and cows be to us happy barbarians here in the good old USA.

To continue: Lt. Brownfelder was shot down, his plane was shot down, I mean to say, and everybody aboard bailed out. Some were captured and some dead on arrival. Flyers were, enemy fliers that is, free game until they hit the ground. The ack-ack puffed around parachutists the same as it did around attacking bombers. After they hit the ground, the German rules of war took immediate effect and they were, for the most part, well treated.

Lt. Brownfelder was looking for graves of lost comrades. He told me one day that the biggest problem he had was language. Although he knew some German, learned in the prison camp, he couldn't really communicate with the villagers about the city.

I volunteered my girlfriend's services as interpreter. She was from Vienna, multilingual, a compassionate soul, needless to say, beautiful, and, for many long years after, my wife. Most important of all to you and Sylvia, she was your mother.

They found the graves, tidily kept in a village here and there. They even found the goddamned airplane in the middle of some small lake submerged in fifty feet of Alpine water.

I suppose it is still there.

The days went on and the search elaborated into the finding of your mother's uncle Eugen, tucked away in some American prison camp in Austria. Poor soul, that one. A retired, leftover general from World War I, called back to service by the theatrics of A. Hitler. He was, it comes to mind, husband of your great-aunt Assunta, blistering away down there now in Salzburg, fantastic people of a long ago age. I have always felt a bit ennobled that it was me who furnished the wheels which eventually led to his freedom. But, again I digress and that's all another story.

The Burgomaster's Truck

Munich

In that vivid summer following the end of the war in Europe happened many things that come frequently to mind. It is now almost twenty-odd years past and scarcely a day goes by that my thoughts are not turned to that strange summer.

A few days ago, I watched Andy Evans put a new muffler on my old car and I got to thinking about the time we delivered fifty two-and-a-half ton trucks to the Burgomaster of Munich. We didn't really get them all delivered. If we had, I probably wouldn't remember the incident at all.

I was dispatcher, PFC, military government, Munich. It was a job of great responsibility. The Colonel told me that himself in his nervous hopeful way. Certainly, it was a job of great status and power. I discovered that myself. In that great wilderness of pedestrians and confusion, I could put anybody on wheels. We all had jobs like that. All eighteen of us. Eighteen people delegated with authority to set up a municipal government in a city of one million or so disenchanted souls. Outrageous authority it was, powered by the conquering armies all over Europe. As I remember it we were most vaguely directed. In all those millions of troops involved in that war, no regiment had more power and less direction than ours. We were a regiment scattered all over Germany, segments of a gigantic authority. The state department later spent years professionalizing what we did off the cuff. I am not sure their present effectiveness is any better, but that's another story.

I was talking about the Burgomaster's trucks. One morning came an unusual directive from the Colonel's office on the second floor. All of them were, now that I think about it. The gist of this directive was, "Go to Bad Homburg, pick up fifty two-and-a-half-ton trucks and deliver them to the Burgomaster of Munich." It was that specific and about that brief. I don't remember it as a memorandum, or a written directive. I think he just called me on the phone. I am sure that our Table of Organization showed someone as my superior officer, but I don't remember who he was. It might have been that captain from a little town in Tennessee who was in charge of the city's fire transportation department. I don't know. I don't recall any conversation with him.

Johnny Cerro was motor sergeant and our approach to the organization matter was simply to act as partners. We supported each other or abandoned each other to whatever problem was current. That time, he abandoned me. His reaction to the directive was simple, "I can't help you. In thirty minutes, I gotta pick up Dorothy Thompson, that woman writer, and drive her to Dachau. She wants to see the ovens. Colonel's orders. GI driver. GI vehicle. No krauts. That silly bastard still hasn't realized he has only seventeen men. Every time some goofy general or US civilian comes through, he acts like he has four or five battalions to order around."

So Johnny left and I called Romeo, who billeted with me, to help. He was assistant to the office in charge of setting up a police department for the city. He was a motorcycle man and could lead a convoy. He had been with the MPs in France during the invasion and how he ever got into our outfit was a mystery. Of course, it was a mystery how any of us got into that outfit. Romeo came to help. Then I called Lieutenant Jordan. Lt. Jordan was the lowest ranking officer in the detachment. He was a Second Lieutenant by rank, but a three-star general when it came to the use of authority. Many stories I can recall about that chap. He told me he would have fifty GI truck drivers report to me in the morning with three trucks to transport them to Bad Homburg. And they did report. They came from various companies of the 45th Infantry Division, which was bivouacked all around Munich impatiently waiting for orders to go home. They were a raunchy set with that big silver-blue infantry badge pinned to their shirts and all feeling randy and lucky to be walking around with the fighting over.

I know how Lt. Jordon got them. He called 45th Division headquarters. He talked to adjutant of that restless outfit, and he said, "This is Military Government Munich. We need fifty qualified men to drive two-and-a-half-ton trucks." And the adjutant said, "Yes, indeed. How many days ration should they carry?" Lt. Jordan said four and hung up the phone. And the adjutant hung up the phone and said, "Hallelujah! At least fifty of these nuts will be out of mischief for four days while we wait for those idiots at GHQ to send shipping orders." Then he sent out a call for fifty volunteers to go to Bad Homburg and drive fifty trucks back to Munich. He took the first lucky fifty to get the message. And they reported to me at 0800 the following morning.

And so did Corporal Romeo J. Betty with his motorcycle. A man with great leadership abilities, assistant to the organizer of the Munich Police department, ready to help. All these years later, I realize that General Patton couldn't have carried out the mission successfully. Not with that crew.

Six days later, Corporal Betty rolled into the courtyard of the Munich Rathaus with his convoy. Five trucks he had. The other forty-eight were lost, strayed, abandoned, stolen, or, as we later learned, sold near the Champs-Élysées in Paris.

It was a vigorous summer.

Romeo was sad and depressed. It was a blow to his ego, to his power of leadership. He told the colonel and me how he got all fifty of the drivers to Bad Homburg. A tremendous feat in itself now that I think about it. Bad Homburg, that huge collection depot where the US armies all over that part of Germany were sending the vehicles now that the war was over and the divisions were being sent home. He told us how he presented his orders for the fifty trucks to some harassed officer who passed him to a weary sergeant who waved his hand to that tremendous park and told him to take any fifty trucks he wanted. He explained his decisiveness in immediately selecting one certain line of trucks, of how he directed his fifty drivers to drive the first fifty trucks that would crank up out onto the autobahn to go two miles and to stop and wait for him. With weariness and a voice full of despair, he unrolled his story. He counted the trucks through the gates, signed the papers for them, cranked up his motorcycle and prepared to take command of the convoy. He had forty-eight trucks in line when he got to the head of the convoy. Five missing. Since there was nothing else to do, he proceeded with the forty-eight. At every village, he lost two or three. Every time the convoy passed a girl on a bicycle, at least one truck developed engine trouble. He solved that particular problem like the born leader he was. He rode ahead and warned any girls he came upon that he headed a convoy with at least three known rapists and advised them they would do well to hide themselves until the convoy passed. Eventually, he lost all but the five he got to Munich with.

Later, in quieter times, we found most of the trucks. They were abandoned in villages all the way back to the Normandy beachhead where the first American soldier met the first European girl.

The Burgomaster of Munich finally got his fifty trucks some months later when things were better organized and less spirited troops occupied the fatherland. To this day, I don't know a single thing about any of the fifty volunteer drivers. But I'm sure they all got home. In those days, a stray GI could always show up in some outfit's chow line with the simple explanation he was hungry and lost from his company.

And the reason this story came to mind when I watched Andy Evans take the old shot muffler off my car was because of a remark Romeo made in his report. He said he had a feeling that he had lost control of the drivers when they cranked up the trucks. He saw about half of those simple clowns get down under the truck while the engines were warming up and methodically and deliberately chop holes in the mufflers so the motors would roar.

"I could see they were wild to go," is what he said.

In-Laws

January 1997

Like the very rich, in-laws are just different. It's a rare Christian that loves and cherishes all his in-laws. Some of them are hard to understand. Some of them are scary. In-law-ship works both ways. You can't have in-laws without being an in-law. My three daughters have married a total of eight times. I am sure I was a kind of scary father-in-law to at least two of those chaps they married—one, for sure. He was gutsy though. He tried not to show his timorousness. Thank God, he drifted on down the road, or out to sea, or whatever. I wonder sometimes what became of him—but I don't wonder long. I just thank God that I knew him but briefly.

I am not a bitter man. In fact, my mind was filled with whimsy when I sat down to write. Over the course of a long and active life, my in-laws have given me much pleasure and good companionship—and good advice, some of which I regret to say, I never took.

I grew up in rural northwest Oklahoma in a standard cohesive family full of aunts and uncles and cousins with no troublesome way of living. I was set loose into the world on my twentieth birthday under the guidance and council of the authorities of the

Army of the United States. At the time, I figured the army would soon avail itself of my capabilities and assign me two or three hundred men, send me to either the Pacific area to clean out the Japanese, or to Europe to rout out the Huns. I expected to be back home in a year or two, and then I would move on to Alaska to seek my fortune.

Four years, eight months, and twenty two days later, I came home. I had a wife and daughter. I had a father-in-law, a mother-in-law, and a brother-in-law. My first in-laws.

When World War II shut down, my father-in-law was imprisoned by the British up in the north of Germany. He was a German naval officer. Actually, he was Austrian. In the First World War, my first father-in-law had been a U-boat captain. A submariner. An Unterseeboot capitan. He may also have served on U-boats during World War II. I don't know. At the end of the war, he was a staff officer for some German Admiral whose name I have forgotten. All German officers of high rank were held prisoners for several months so that the Allies could investigate their background and activities in the Nazi party. Like most German prisoners, he was released and sent home, but because of his high officer standing, he was restricted to menial labor. He accepted this without any complaint or comment that I ever heard and went dutifully to work as a gardener.

It never changed his personality in the least. On his way to his garden job in the early morning, he walked down the steps from his apartment building to the street with all the erectness and alertness of an admiral coming ashore from his flagship. No matter what he was wearing, he could create the illusion that he was still in uniform. From a hundred yards, you would know that he was a military man of the officer class.

He was a smallish man with a swarthy complexion. He had more hair on his eyebrows than he had on his head. The eyebrows stood out like little shelves above his black eyes. They may not have been black. Dark brown and shiny more likely. When he got to be about ninety years old, his eyes sparkled. When he was younger, his eyes gleamed.

While he was in prison in the British Sector, his wife frequently wrote to him. When he got his second or third letter from his spouse at home in Munich, he learned that his little girl (she was eighteen) was not only working for the Yanks as an interpreter, but was also fraternizing with a Yank soldier, who came frequently to his house.

I don't remember much discussion about what he might have thought about all this. After all, he was on the losing end of two great wars, he was a prisoner, and then comes word that his only daughter is very friendly with a soldier of the conquerors. When he finally came home and we met in his house, he greeted me cordially; and he treated me that way all of his life. He would like to have discussed with me the reasons for the two great world wars, but it was difficult because our interpreter, his daughter, looked upon the whole subject as total idiocy. She pretty much established a mental block on the subject of war. Which of course, is one way of moving on.

My first father-in-law gave me advice only one time that I recall. It was a little German rhyme he spoke to me on the morning my first child (his first grandchild) was born. It translates to this meaning: "To become a father is no big thing. To be a father is a big thing." I have recalled it to mind several times down through the years.

Chaotic Times: Trip to Pirano in 1945

Written 1996-1997

The events of this tale occurred fifty one years ago in the early fall following the close of the war in Europe May 8, 1945.

I was young, strong, vigorous, full-grown, intelligent, ignorant, unblemished, and confident. I was, after all, a corporal of the conquering army, and I had a wonderful job laden with power and prestige. The prestige derived considerably from my civilian assistant translator, a young Austrian *fraulein* from Vienna, an educated lassie caught up at the end of the war living in Munich with her mother and little brother, waiting for her papa to come home from a British prison camp up in Hamburg.

The mother of this *madchen* was an Adomovitch whose family had spent their long summers between the wars, in the village of Pirano on the Adriatic Sea, south of Trieste.

And the mother said to me one evening in her living room where we were sipping tea and nibbling a black bread lathered with US Army issue orange marmalade, "I vunder lieber, Mac, about our house in Pirano. I wonder if it is still there. It has been so many years since I had news from there."

"Where is Pirano?"

"It is in Yugoslavia near the city of Trieste in Italy, and I heard this morning that the Yanks and the Tommies both occupy Trieste now."

"The French are there too, Muttie."

"Ach. The French. What difference do the French make? Here, there, anywhere. The French!" She was not a frankophile.

"Perhaps," she continued, while tipping a bit of scotch into my hot tea, "You could drive your jeep down there with die Maria and see if the house is still there. Maria speaks Italian fluently. Mr. Marconi, the maker of the radio, visited us at that house one time when Maria was just a tiny girl. You remember him, don't you, liebling?"

"Ach...well, it was a long time ago. You could drive down through Austria. It is so beautiful this time of year, and the Yanks, they are camped everywhere from here to there all through Austria and Italy, down to Trieste where the Britishers are camped. Die var is fertig, over, it would be safe!"

So Corporal Davis and his official translator went to Trieste on temporary duty orders for seven days with the Military

Government Detachment in Trieste, Italy. Authorization for the jeep incorporated in the orders. I do not remember how this was all arranged—the papers and the orders, and the permits. I do remember the major saying, when he handed me the orders and the permits, "Well, Davis, the colonel signed them...pretty good duty, eh, corporal? Don't get lost. Come back with the jeep and the civilian. Seven days plus travel time."

"Certainly, Sir. I'll follow the orders. We'll be back on time." Maybe. They were nice guys, the colonel and the major. They liked us. We were capable. I never did find the outfit in Trieste that I was temporarily assigned to. I remember deciding that it didn't even exist. Of course, we never spent much time looking for it.

Those were chaotic times. The colonel and the major of our outfit were not really military people. They were civilian specialists commissioned and sent to Germany to do a specific job at the close of hostilities. The sergeant, and the corporals, the NCOs were the militaristic, the catch-one-quick kids who figured out how to make things work. How to move the fuel, the food, the vehicles, the people from here to there, etc.

We left in the early morning with four extra jerry cans of gasoline strapped on the bumpers and a bag full of rations and other negotiables and necessaries. It was indeed a lovely day.

At the border crossing checkpoint near Salzburg, the US sergeant checked the papers—all the papers. He smiled at my sweet faced companion. He smiled at me and said, "Pretty good duty, eh, Corporal?"

"Yes. I like it." And I smiled too.

He handed me back the papers. "You have one problem," he said, and he was no longer smiling. "Our orders emphasize that no civilian in a military vehicle can pass through without CIC clearance clearly stamped on all her documents. No exception, Corporal. Our Lieutenant is young and green and fresh from West Point. No exceptions."

"So. How do we get clearance...where is the CIC?"

"Back in the last village there are two agents. One of them shacks up in a little blue house on the north side of the square. They both wear spook type trench coats. If you see one of them, you'll know him."

I saw him on the very first trip around the square—trench coat and all, staggering along.

"Hey buddy, I'm looking for the CIC Can you help me?"

"Yes," he said, "I can. I am it."

"We need CIC clearance to pass into Austria. We have orders to Trieste."

Then the most astonishing thing happened. The man reached into his coat pocket, pulled out a rubber stamp with a wooden handle, staggered over to the jeep hood and said, "Lay your documents here on the hood."

He stamped every paper we laid out. He looked at the girl and smiled. He looked at me and smiled. "You are obviously a lucky man," he said.

"So are you, my friend," said I and poked a half-liter bottle of Vermouth into his trench coat pocket.

Twenty minutes later at the check point, the sergeant looked carefully at all the stamped documents.

"You're quick," he said, "and thorough too. That is the only vehicle trip ticket I' have ever seen with a CIC clearance stamped on it. Pass through."

"So long, Sergeant. I'll see you next week."

"No you won't. I ship out for home tomorrow."

Saga of WWII: Letter to the Editor, *Fairview Republican*

This is the story of two heroic brothers (front-page header in *Fairview Republican*). It was written in response to a request for a story about a local hero. August 31, 1995.

Dear Editor,

The *Random House Dictionary* defines the word hero in this way: "A man of distinguished courage or ability, admired for his brave deeds and noble qualities." Heroes exist in all walks of life. We all know a few people of that caliber.

In World War II, it was not a professional military force that was victorious. It was a force of fifteen million armed citizens that prevailed in that miserable chaos, some of them surviving pain and suffering with unimaginable endurance.

Here is a story of two brothers from this community who went together into that war. It was a well-known story forty to fifty years ago. It is worth repeating today. Here is the bare outline of it.

In January 1944, Joe David Howerton, twenty-nine; and his brother, Everett Howerton, thirty-three, were called into the army. They were both married. Joe David had two children. Everett had three.

The Howerton brothers were sent to a camp for basic training in the infantry. Infantry (duty) was a high priority in January 1944. Within a few months, they were in Europe and assigned to the ninety-fourth Infantry Division, part of Patton's army, the army that moved fast. Both of them were assigned to the same platoon.

In a fight following the Battle of the Bulge, they were sent forward with forty-three other men to wipe out a German pillbox. Caught in a cross-fire and in a mine field, they retreated.

Five men got back to cover. The rest did not. Joe David had seen Everett step on a mine, so when darkness fell, he crawled back toward the pillbox to find his brother.

"Everett's foot was gone and he had a head wound. He was delirious. I had to hold him down to get the morphine into him and a tourniquet." (Note: all infantry men carried morphine tablets.)

"How did you carry him out, Joe David?"

"I straddled him on my hands and knees and told him to lock his arms around my neck. Crawling, I drug him back. It was almost daylight when we got back to the company. I helped strap him on the ambulance jeep. The jeep carried three stretchers. The medics gave us whiskey to relax us. Told us to drink all we wanted. It was a cold day, February 19, and we were sweating."

At 1:00 p.m. on that same day, Joe David went forward again with his company. That time, they had tank support and the mission was successful. He fought for three more months.

"At Dusseldorf, we had a hard, hard time. Our last fight was on May 1 near Mannheim. Then we veered south, and when it stopped on May 8, we were in Czechoslovakia."

Altogether, he was one hundred days on the line, attacking or defending against fire. "I went sixty-two days without changing clothes. I was never hit. I don't know why."

When it was over, Joe David and one other soldier, a Carl Sellers, were the only men left of the original platoon. They came home when it was over, Joe David and Everett Howerton, and went back to work.

Everett died in 1986. As far as I know, he never retired. He did carpentry work, drove trucks, drove tractors, and mechanized—fixed things all his life. He stumped around for forty years on a plastic foot and never cut himself any slack.

Joe David moved to Enid after the war and became a house painter. "I've painted over a thousand houses," he told me, "Some both inside and outside."

He lives now in the nursing home here in Fairview. He has had three strokes and he suffers with arthritis. He is bedfast. If you visit him in the afternoon, he might talk with you.

Do I look upon the Howerton brothers as heroes? Indeed, I do.

War Time Memories (Letter)

At home in Major County, August 24, 1987

Dear Ones,

    We have had several days of coolish weather, cloudy, and, last night, a rain. So I am in the house doing deskwork, which I, with some guilt, put off as long as I can. Just now, I decided I must really set all this dreary stuff aside and write a cheery letter to the children in far-off Japan. Who would have ever thought I would have a daughter teaching school in Japan? Forty-odd years ago, I could have understood the possibility (I could have been sent to the Pacific, you see, rather than the European war etc.). Anyway, Yusuke and Tom are home safely as we have been notified by one telephone call and two letters. It was a most interesting visit and they are really fine lads. When we got home from Ft. Worth after putting them on the plane, Kay fell into bed and slept for thirteeen hours. She is so determined that visitors must be enthralled with every single minute in her house that she about drives herself frazzled. She was beginning to look upon them as her own children. I am sure it was and will be a good thing for everybody involved—parents, children, teacher, friends etc.

    Your remarks about the Hiroshima Day observation was understandable, but I always have offsetting thoughts and observations which balance out the horror, or something. I don't know if you can really balance out horror. Violence. When they dropped the bomb and the war stopped, Truman justified it with estimates of how many lives, both American and Japanese had been saved by bringing the war to an instant close. And when you talk with people who fought in the Pacific, they all are pleased they didn't have to invade Japan and slaughter through millions of people. It all seems so far away most of the time (the war), but then again, it can all come rushing back into my mind with some casual remark or some fleeting thought and it is like it was just yesterday that we were all geared up to wipe out the bad guys and preserve things for the good guys. For instance, I am not very active in the American Legion, but once in awhile, I do affiliate myself with them. First, I must say that veterans do not sit around talking about their service time or tell war stories. They eat, drink, and play cards and look at their watches often to see if it is time to be home. Another thing they do, at least in this community, is go through a little ritual at veterans' funerals when requested by the family. Frequently, they serve as pall bearers. The ritual consists of ten or twelve guys getting into a kind of uniform and going out to the cemetery where the coffin is draped with an American flag. When the preachers and the singers are all through and they are ready to drop the coffin, two (sometimes four) vets step up, retrieve the flag, fold it precisely thus and so into a triangular package and present it to the most bereaved—mother, wife, child, sister, whoever—with a salute. Meanwhile, the rest of the detail stands nearby at attention with rifles held at the position of present arms. Two fellows support flags, large flags, socketed in a harness affair slung from their shoulders. After the flag is presented to the most bereaved, the sergeant-at-arms barks out a series of orders which result in the bugler sounding out the call "Taps." The bugler is usually not visible. He is some distance away. Today it is usually a guy with an amplifier and a tape crouched behind some cedar bushes or a large tombstone. When the bugler finishes—it is an eerie sound and, sometimes, quite moving, the riflemen point their firearms skyward and fire three volleys. It is shatteringly loud and brings the ceremony to a definite and positive end.

 This seems like a long introduction to the story I set out to tell. It is a long introduction. And now, it is time for lunch. So during lunch, I will try to recall what it was I was going to tell you when I started telling you something.

 So now it is ten in the evening, and I just read what I have written and I find that I was on the verge of relating a "for instance" story.

Two days after Yusuke and Tomatsu are gone, and we are still kind of loosely allied with Japanese culture, I am asked to help with the funeral of an old school mate and friend Dallas Howerton. A fellow who worked here on the farm for Uncle Dawson back when I was a kid of thirteen and he was a kid of seventeen. So ten or twelve of us gather in the Legion hut that morning about an hour before the funeral to get suited up and dig out the rifles and the blank cartridges and the flags and so forth. It is always pretty casual and a kind of fumbling, disorganized milling around affair sorting out the gear and repeating tired old jokes about big bellies in uniform and somebody always asks, "Does anybody remember how to load this damn thing and where is the safety catch?" No mourning, no awe, everybody has been through it many times. When everything is more or less ready, some of us walk over to the church to attend the funeral while the others take the paraphernalia out to the cemetery, which is where our part of the business takes place. In this church we sit together in a pew, the six or seven vets, and wait and listen and meditate like everybody else. Then we go out of the church first and hurry on out to the cemetery so we will be all set up when the rest of the people get there.

The story I am getting to is back up there where we are milling around getting out the gear. The rifles are kept in a locked cabinet and the helmets, light weight plastic things, set on a shelf. The helmets are white. Enameled. Dusty. Frank Koehn is dusting a helmet with a dust cloth. "Man!" he says, "I just remember, a shiny helmet is what got me shot up by those Japanese." It was a thought that hadn't crossed his mind in years. You could tell that. So could everybody else. For a few seconds, everyone was quiet, a little startled even. Then someone chuckled, and I said, "How did that happen Frank? Where were you?" And before he knew, it he was telling a story, a war story, his story. And he kept rubbing the helmet with the dust cloth.

"On the island of Luzon we were moving through the brush in the night and it was raining. About a mile or so away, there was an airstrip and the turning light from the tower flashed across us and they saw our shiny, wet helmets bobbing up and down in the brush and they followed us. Somebody figured all that out after it was over. They followed us and when we went into bivouac they sneaked up on us—when the shooting began, it came from everywhere. When they hit me, I was standing up and the blood was running out of both my sleeves. I headed for the medic's hole (foxhole). I jumped right in on top of him and damn near drowned him, mashed him right down in the mud and water."

Then Frank put on his helmet, tossed the dustcloth to someone else and we went on getting ready for the funeral.

Walking to the church to attend the funeral, I was thinking about that story and it crossed my mind that maybe Yusuke's grandfather saw those shiny helmets bobbing in the brush one rainy night on the Island of Luzon. Maybe, etc.

Nine o'clock next morning, and it is an absolutely windless, bright sunny morning with heavy dew glistening on the grass.

The farming goes along just fine. It has been a wet summer which makes things easier in a way: not so wet I can't work in the fields but just about right so that I can keep the ground in good shape. Will be sowing wheat in two or three weeks. Starting, at least. I string it out for quite awhile you know. Have only a small amount of maize this year, twenty-eight acres. Last year had 120. Government program! Also have about a hundred acres of cowpeas. Chinese reds and red rippers. Little red bean things. One pound of dried red beans will do us for a year. I'm not sure what I can do with thousands of pounds, The market is slow on red beans. Oh well, they will build up the soil so we can raise more wheat!

Take care. Stay loose. Enjoy the day. Save your money. Buy land. Don't shove any beans up your nose.

Love, M.

Rue du Larue

English II, Mr. Thornton
University of Oklahoma, Feb. 5, 1948

When one creeps forth in the early hours of the morning from one of the cheap little cafés that clutter the Rue du Larue, suffering the miseries of overindulgence and dissipation, the street presents a sad spectacle for one's tired eyes. The tightly shuttered shop windows, the feeble glow of the street lights, and the isolated, narrow, winding street overwhelms and depresses one with lonesomeness and despondency. The reek of the ancient gutters and the filth on the damp, uneven cobblestones assault one's very soul. And as one fumbles along that foul, dark, crooked, and uneven little street, all of the evil of the world seems to be descending on the Rue du Larue.

It is, however, not always so, for on a bright, sunny afternoon, when the cares of the day have passed, and the troubles of tomorrow are in the faraway future, the street becomes one of the nicer habitats of man. It is a stream, flowing with representatives of every type of humanity, dotted with islands of sidewalk cafés, and banked by gay, picturesque little shops. It is a living thing, peopled with living things: with pretty girls busily going nowhere, with long-skirted old women peddling chestnuts and cheap candy, with waiters leisurely polishing the diminutive tops of the sidewalk tables, with nonchalant taxi drivers lounging around their vehicles. The effervescent atmosphere of the Rue du Larue penetrates all of its inhabitants; they smile and chatter to one another as they saunter along the quaint street. And the smiles, the pleasant chattering, the gay laughter of the people make one feel that all the contentment of the world is centered in the Rue du Larue.

Poems by Mac Davis

Anvil from Missouri
(December 31, 1977)

A piece of steel on my headchute
Bent out of a shape the other day
When I tried to trap a steer
And some mechanism hung tight

This morning I took it off
And took it to my shop
To fix it up
To weld it and reinforce it

The curve of the bend
Yielded to no special tool on hand
So I took the rod and a great big hammer
Out to the back of the shed

And I pounded it all straight
On a hunk of iron that's laid there
All my life.

A hunk of iron
Hauled down from Missouri
By my grandfather
Eighty years ago

A heavy hunk of iron
Out of some old cornmeal mill
And the thought came to me
As I knelt there in the dirt

How many Davises have hammered out
Some bent up thing on this old hunk of iron
A right good many
Is what I thought.

Uncle Jacob

Strong Man
Asthmatic Child
Trumpet Man
Leader of the Band
Oldest Son
Father Dead at thirty-two
Mother-reared
Farmer
Strong Man
Lift a loaded header barge
The rear end of a tractor
A wagon load of sand
Soldier
Grain Dealer
Grocery Man
Cotton Ginner
Father Man
Electric Light Plant Man
Miller of Wheat
Seller of Flour
Hard Man
Soft Man
Farmer
Grower of Wheat
Harvester
Oklahoma to Montana
Hog-raiser

Cattleman
Grandpa Man
Never-work-for-any-man
Strong Man
Dead by Accident

Bill McCue

My grandfather
Bill McCue
Is now long dead
I remember him well
An enigma and delight
For instance
His reading habits
Confusing to a child
By his chair
Were books
Stacked from the floor
To the top of his smoking stand
Another enigma
An island of chaos
In a ship-shape house
But the books
All interlaced
With dime store Western pulps
Frowned-on reading
By church and school
Heavy stuff
By any standard
Shakespeare
Boswell
Oklahoma Statutes
Old Testament
Things like that

A sense of history
I got from him
I now know
From slight remarks
Encompassing
Perhaps a minute
Sixty seconds
One had to do
With an event as sheriff
In a Kansas County
In nineteen-oh-something
And the other had to do
With I don't know what
But it was brief
The other thing
I remember
From him
Ignoring all personalities
He liked to
God bless him
Pin down things
To persons
But not always
One time
He told me
Or perhaps it was my father
He told it to
To make a living
A man must work
To make a good living
A man must work hard
To make money
A man must do
Something else.

Buzzards

The buzzards fly
To where the dying lie
They circle and wait
Until the dying die
Then they drop
To where the dead things lie

Lines on a Mantis

Mantis drawing

In artful ways
The mantis preys
Upon the life around her
Fragile as a leaf
Procryptic hued
Stilted in a swaying stance
Prayerful ballerina
Bulb eyed head
Passing slowly to and fro
Voracious bug
Pugnacious thugs
Saw-toothed sabers

To lash and draw
Set in form devotional
And quick as light
There is no fight
Brings she the meal to her
Procryptic hued
With stealth imbued
She views the life around her
Stilted in a swaying stance
Quiet as a leaf
Procryptic hued
Brown-green stick bug
Voracious thug
Swivel necked
With swan like grace
Quiet as a leaf
A Durer pose
Bulb-eyed head
To and fro
Prayerful pose
Web like grace
Ballerina
Watutsi
à la Durer

Tranquil

February 1979

I walked out
Onto my porch
In stockinged feet
The snow was damp
And my feet got cold
I looked around

I looked about
I saw my barns
I saw my cattle
The barns were tight
My cattle were quiet
Filled with my own hay
And sweet water
From the wells
The dogs were fed
The cats were fed
The birds were fed
With seed wheat cleanings
Cheap stuff-indeed
My feet got colder
Soppy, freezing they were
It all looked pretty good to me
Tranquil is the word
So I went back into the house
And put on dry socks

A Man of Color (Janruary 20, 1997)

He was a true blue greenhorn
No yellow streak
A redneck black from Brownsville
Without pinko politics, or red-ass attitude,
Nor grey demeanor,
More, like, crystal clear
And, all in all
A real white man.

Masked Beauty (March 10, 1968)

Sylvia Davis (1950-2006)

The beauty of a young girl
Hidden and masked
In the enigma
Of a puzzled mind
Aloof, cautious, sedate, precise
Guarding
Against intrusion
With a self
All held together
By a supreme
Power of will
Electroshock
And
A precise dosage
Of medicants
Carefully ingested
Every four hours

Alcohol Poem (November 10, 1968)

Drink is not the irrational
Quality of my life
Stone-cold sober sanity
Reality, awareness
Is my special form
Of madness
The illusions of civilized souls
Have faded and disappeared
For me
The ancient skeptic
The constant observer
The forever duty-bound
The worker
The doer
The knower
And fixer of unworking things
Is mad
Hopelessly mad
At conflict
With the illusions
Of civilization
And unable
To do
Anything
Vitality wanes
Youth is wasting
Drink
Alky
Rebirths the mind
For one blazing hour
To beauty
And rests the body
In deathly numbness

For five hours
So that it may rise up again
To dare the madness
Raging
Everywhere

A postscript added twelve years later:

When I stopped drinking
I became the man
I always knew
I was.

Commentaries About McWilliam Davis

To the Family and Friends of McWilliam Davis from Skip Hulett, Mac's Nephew

Read at funeral, June 12, 1997

Neither the sun nor death can be looked at steadily. I suppose it is a flaw of human nature to take for granted those events and persons that seem so solid, so steady; those who have always been there for us. McWilliam Davis was my grandfather and grandmother's oldest child and only son. He was my mother's brother, my uncle. He was the rock and anchor of our family. He was stories.

Mac has always been about stories. When I was a small child, it was stories about him, wondrous tales of far-away places, far-away events, far-away people. As I grew older, it was the stories he himself told by pen or by word; stories and tales of community, of friends, of common, and not-so-common occurrences; stories of the past and the present; stories of successes, of failures, of human flaws, of human greatness, stories of humor, and sadness—stories of living. Tales that captured and held us, that have become a part of each of us, that we carry and remember, that cause us to laugh, to think, to wonder; words that inspire and comfort us; words and thoughts that will always remain with us.

I have often wondered how he could take the most common and mundane of events and weave them with his own words and spellbind us. Retelling his stories to others never had the same effect, never captured others as we had been captured. Thus, I came to realize that Mac's stories were all parables: all had a moral or inspirational message, and the truth was not found in the stories but in the storyteller.

His life was an allegory—of goodness, of morality, good nature, good humor, forgiveness, love; of acceptance and tolerance; of honesty and character. He was, and remains, an inspiration to all.

He was a gentleman and a gentle man; and in perfect keeping with his character, he did go gentle into that good night and did not rage against the dying of the light.

I have always been secretly proud when in the common confusion of keeping familial identities straight, my grandfather, grandmother, mother, or aunt would occasionally mistakenly address me as "Mac." I felt for a moment I had lived up to something terribly good, wonderful, and special.

I miss him terribly.
H. P. White "Skip"
Placentia, Belize
June 11, 1997

To the Family and Friends of McWilliam Davis from Carrie Hulett, Mac's Niece

Davis Family

Uncle Mac was the patriarch of the Davis-McCue family after Granddaddy's death, and he held that position quite well. To me, he truly exhibited the best qualities of his parents, Fred E. Davis and Hazel McCue Davis, and their families.

From the Davis clan he received a love of farming and the land, the value of hard work, and the enjoyment of a bountiful table. I will always associate family gatherings with good food and lots of it.

From the McCue clan, he acquired his love of reading and his wonderful ability to write and tell stories.

Mac was a great communicator in his own, special way. He could make a story about anything fascinating. Who else could make a story about a tractor interesting to a city girl? He was a great observer of the people and things around him and could converse about any subject. He could always see the humor in any situation. Also, he was good listener.

Mac was a giving and understanding man. The home he and Kay had was warm and loving. Everyone felt welcome there.

I feel so fortunate to have family members both who were farmers and who actually lived on the farm. It enriched my life as a child and as an adult. It is a joy to watch my sons visit "The Farm" with so much enthusiasm.

I miss him and his presence, but he will live on in the hearts and memories of many.

Goodbye, Mac Davis

From the Editor of the Fairview Republican. June 12, 1997

Fairview, Major County, and I all lost a great friend this week. Mac Davis was one of those rare men who always had a good word and optimistic view of life-sardonic sense of humor. Mac was a gentleman farmer. He got his hands dirty with the best of them, but washed up often and came to town for more important projects. History was one of his first passions. He almost single-handedly revived a failing Major County Historical Society. He did the personal work necessary for Augusta Specht to donate a quarter of land and over $100,000 to start the museum. Mac recruited the people to organize the first threshing bee, and served as president of the Historical Society for several years. He always had a yarn about the history of this area, or knew someone who did. When I first moved to Fairview, Mac and Kay were solid sources of information, upon whom I relied on a great deal. They continued to be sources of story ideas or project ideas or musings, great and small. Many may not remember that Mac and Kay have a tie to this newspaper. Both have worked here from time to time, Mac, most recently, as a guest columnist. After rereading some of the last he wrote before he quit writing, I had to wonder if maybe that tractor might not occasionally have served as a hiding place from his wife.

Goodbye, Mac. We'll miss you.

Complete Obituary for Mac Davis

Fairview Republican. June 10, 1997

Mac Davis died June 8, 1997 at Fairview Hospital. Funeral services will be at 2pm at the Fairview Mennonite Brethren Church. Burial will be at the Davis family farm southeast of Fairview.

Mac was born Jan 20, 1923 to Fred E. and Hazel McCue Davis. His grandparents settled on the farm in 1898. The land is being farmed now by the fourth generation of Davises with help from the fifth generation.

He grew up in the Fairview community, attended Progressive School and Fairview schools, graduating from Fairview High School. He and his cousin Bob attended one semester of college at Alva before Mac enlisted in the Army in 1942, serving two tours of duty in Europe. While serving with the military government in Munich, Germany he met and married Maria Pospischil. They had two children, Assunta and Sylvia. After the war, Mac bought a house in Norman and a Baldwin combine in Fairview and attended Oklahoma University for four years, spending the summers custom harvesting with his uncle and cousins. He graduated with a degree in Geology and moved to Kensington, Maryland, where he did mapping work for the Army for a time before he and two partners started their own mapping company, Photogrammetry, Inc.

Mac married Kay Moore in Maryland, and they later moved to Fairview with their two children, Tanya and Jesse in 1961. He worked for the Major County ASCS office for several years before devoting all his time to farming. He farmed both in Fairview and Eads, Colorado, and spent many enjoyable hours traveling to Eads with Jake Boehs. Mac and Kay extended many of their trips to Eads to the mountains for short vacations.

Mac was instrumental in re-activating the Major County Historical Society and served as president for several terms. He was a member of American Legion Post 51, a past member of the Breakfast Lions Club. He was a life-long member of the Methodist Church, was a member of the Los Amigos Sunday school class, which he taught from time to time.

His favorite gifts, both to give and receive, were books. He was a scholar, reading avidly, and was very knowledgeable on a wide range of subjects. History was a particular favorite, and he could recount stories from any period.

Mac wrote a weekly column, "Notes from a Farmer", for the Fairview Republican for several years. His stories were entertaining and thoughtful, and were looked forward to by his fans. His letters to family and friends were just as eagerly anticipated, and his character and humor came through as clearly on an e-mail message as a hand-written note.

He found interest wherever he was, but his favorite place to travel and relax was Belize, where he and Kay went a number of times and had many friends. He enjoyed relaxing on the beach, spending many hours reading there.

Mac's favorite place was home. When Kay and his children and grandchildren were there, he was happiest. Mac and Kay's house was a gathering place for not only his family but for many, many people to whom he was friend and mentor.

He will be missed.

Surviving him are his wife, Kay, one son, Jesse and his wife Calleen, of Fairview; three daughters, Assunta Martin and her husband Augie, in Nagasaki, Japan, Sylvia Smith and her husband Ron, of Hunter, and Tanya Robinett and her husband Melvin, of Canton; two sisters, Frances Hulett of Oklahoma City, and Virginia Hall and her husband Don, of Tulsa; and five grandchildren, Angela Davis, Kelsey Kennedy, Nicole Davis, Elijah Kennedy, and Warburton MacKinnon.

He was preceded in death by his parents and one brother.

Note: *Because the very large number of people who attended Mac's funeral could not be accommodated by the smaller Methodist Church, the more spacious Fairview Mennonite Brethren Church graciously came to the rescue.*